"One of our most important discoveries has been the restorative nature of a number of the venues, places that can uplift and inspire your spirit and leave you with a sense of well-being, for instance, a certain spot in a museum, a vista by the river or at the ocean, a garden, a fountain or outdoor sculpture, the exterior of an innovative building, or a particularly beautiful interior."

Grace & Jacqueline

Loving LA

The Low Carbon Way

A Personal Guide to the City of the Angels via Public Transportation

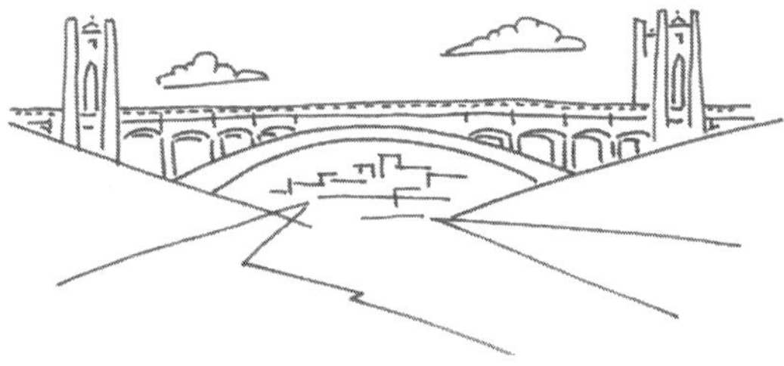

Grace E. Moremen & Jacqueline Chase

Photographs by Grace E. Moremen
Drawings by Ronald T. Evans

LovingLA.com

updates • addenda • corrections
color • scale • links • comments
adventures • so much more

Claremont California
2015

Published by
Dream Boat Press
768 Plymouth Road
Claremont, California 91711
USA

Book Design by Michael Kirk

Cover photos by Grace E. Moremen

Interior photos by Grace E. Moremen
with single contributions by Michael G. Witmer
and Jllm06 (Wikimedia)

Drawings by Ronald T. Evans

Maps and Information Design by Michael Kirk

Epilogue verse from the song "City of the Angels"
by Grace E. Moremen © 2010

ISBN-13 978-1508805830
ISBN-10 1508805830

The publisher and the authors have made every effort to provide accurate, up-to-date information at the time of publication; neither the publisher nor the authors assume any responsibility for errors or changes that occur after publication. Further, the publisher and authors accept no responsibility for loss or injury sustained by any person using this book.

PRINTED IN THE UNITED STATES OF AMERICA by CreateSpace, North Charleston, South Carolina

Dedicated to all our loved ones,
especially our mothers, Agnes and Bernadette,
who shared their love of big cities with us

ACKNOWLEDGMENTS

We are most grateful to the following:

David Oxtoby • President of Pomona College, for giving this project his full support and for graciously writing the Foreword.

Marylou Ferry • Vice President for Communications, and Sneha Abraham, Assistant Director News and Strategic Content, Pomona College for their invaluable help.

Michael Kirk • for his creative book design, image editing, and the forthcoming ebook editions and website.

Michael Hyatt • for his finishing touches.

Ronald T. Evans • for his delightful drawings and his perspective on the project.

Nancy Swearer • for her many hours of invaluable copy editing.

Connie Kimos • for her expert proofreading.

Catherine Banbury • for her suggestions and for creating the title for the book.

Paddy Calistro • for taking our book seriously and making many creative suggestions.

Robert D. Herman • for talking with us about his extremely useful and pioneering book, *Downtown Los Angeles, A Walking Guide.*

Anthony and **Nicole Brooks** • Claremont Camera and Video, for their skill in scanning and transferring over 400 of Grace's photographs to disk.

Rosie Lee Hooks • Director of the Watts Towers Cultural Center, for taking time to share information with us about the Towers and the Center.

The Transportation Committee at Pilgrim Place • for their enthusiastic support of the book.

Michael G. Witmer • for giving us a personal tour of downtown LA, and for taking our picture by City Hall.

J. Eric Lynxwiler • for his expert guidance and enthusiasm on the Neon Cruise, and for his gracious endorsement of our book.

Rhonda Diaz • for showing us the "Mercadito" and for her gracious endorsement of the book.

The LA Conservancy • for endorsing our book and for their informative tours of downtown LA.

The LA Chinatown Business Improvement Association • for providing the helpful walking tour of Chinatown.

The Los Angeles Department of Cultural Affairs • for expanding our knowledge of the historic beginnings of Los Angeles by providing a free walking tour of the Old Plaza and Olvera Street.

Helen Turner • for suggesting that we visit the LA Flower Market.

Jeanne Halverson • for first introducing us to the LA River Greenway.

Louilyn Hargett and **Leslie Ortick** • for sharing their information about the Church of Christian Fellowship, United Church of Christ.

Yvette LaVigne • for generously taking time to show us around the West Adams District.

Sonia Laurens • for her warm hospitality at the Peace Awareness Center.

Sylvia Shen and **Angela Donnelly** • for translating the Chinese characters on the banners at the Museum of Chinese American History.

Saul • our waiter at the Biltmore Hotel, who kindly served us tea on the Royal Albert china.

Angela Donnelly, Sue Mayfield, Lynne Juarez, and **Janet Vandevender** • our cheerful companions on some of the Adventures.

Chris Chase and **William Moremen** • for their unfailing encouragement regarding the book, and for faithfully transporting us to and from the Metrolink station, and to canine "**Max**" for his joyous welcomes.

And, finally, **Metrolink**, the **Los Angeles County Metropolitan Transportation Authority (MTA)**, and the **Los Angeles Department of Transportation (LADOT)** without whose buses and trains—operated by their skilled, patient drivers and conductors—this project would not have been possible.

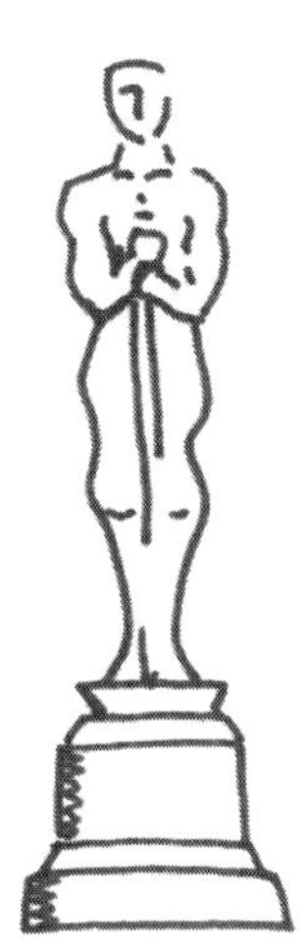

IN·THE·WORLD·OF
AFFAIRS·WE·LIVE·IN·OUR
OWN·AGE·IN·BOOKS
WE·LIVE·IN·ALL·AGES

FOREWORD

In their delightfully informative book, *Loving LA the Low Carbon Way*, Grace Moremen and Jacqueline Chase show readers that contrary to popular perception Los Angeles isn't only about cars—a sizeable chunk of the landmarks in the City of Angels can also be seen by foot, rail, bike, and bus.

All of the 24 trips they recommend and meticulously detail are paeans to the megalopolis, woven through with history and insider tips that will inspire natives, transplants, and visitors alike to set out and experience it for themselves—whether taking in the murals of East LA, the Los Angeles River, or the treasures of Bunker Hill.

I came to Los Angeles in 2003 to serve as president at Pomona College, located in tree-lined Claremont just a few dozen miles away from the heart of downtown Los Angeles and mere steps away from the local Metrolink station. Upon my arrival, one of my first charges to our students was the "47 Things" challenge—must-do activities and trips that are uniquely Southern Californian and should be experienced before graduation. My other charge is for Pomona to be a leader in sustainability. The vast majority of our students don't have cars, so *Loving LA the Low Carbon Way* will be the perfect green guide for them to navigate this great city without one.

This guide is certainly for anyone who wants to learn about Los Angeles; this city companion book offers a breadth and depth of knowledge and planning quite unlike any other I've read.

I was raised in Pennsylvania, schooled in Massachusetts and Northern California, and worked in Chicago prior to coming to LA. I have found it has a wholly unique vibrancy and, thanks to this book, more immediacy and accessibility than I knew. Los Angeles may indeed, as they say, have been built around the automobile, yet with some creativity and forethought it can be enjoyed without one. Before I even finished chapter one, I was ready to lace up my walking shoes, charge up my Metro card, and with *Loving LA the Low Carbon Way* in hand, re-explore and re-imagine the region I have come to call home.

David Oxtoby
January 21, 2015

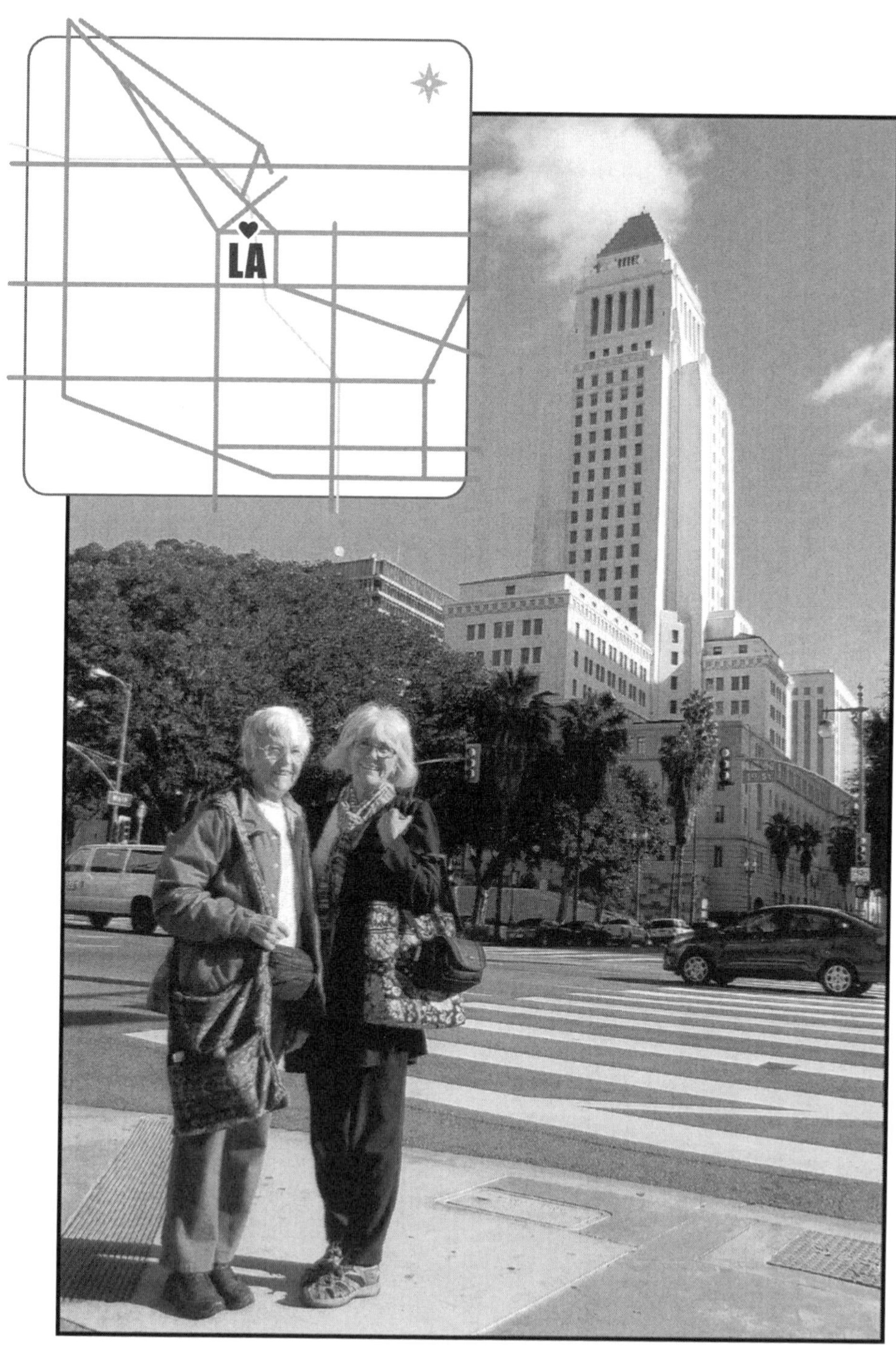
LA

WHY WE LOVE LA

Grace: I love the bigness of LA. I like the feeling of being enveloped by the city.

LA is where I was born and grew up. But I feel that it is everybody's city, and that no matter where we have come from, or where we live now, we can all belong to this City of the Angels. There is room for endless diversity. I love the physical beauty of LA, its majestic mountains and sun drenched beaches, its boulevards that stretch out to the Pacific Ocean, its lights at night that seem to spread to infinity.

I cannot say that I love all the *history* of LA—too many decisions along the way have resulted in tragedy and injustice. But I honor its tiny beginnings, and I respect its honest growing pains as it has coped with earthquakes, floods, and sociopolitical upheavals. Today I applaud its rebirth as a modern city while it makes its beauty and resources more accessible to people in various ways—better public transportation, "re-greening" the LA River, and reinvesting in some of the older neighborhoods. Most of all, I love the energy of LA. And I defy any other city in the world to match LA's endless inventiveness, its boundless creativity, its optimism, or its ardent hope for a better future.

Jacqueline: I am falling in love with LA. Prior to beginning the LA project with Grace, I had been intimidated by the extensive freeway system and the traffic, even though I had been born in, and loved, another great city. I did not realize that the gems of this city, many hidden in plain sight, could be revealed.

New York City, where I was born and grew up until my late teens, is definitely a touchstone for me. My earliest memories are of the vitality and neighborliness of Greenwich Village, when that was a working-class, multicultural neighborhood, where people watched out for each other. I walked to grade school, and later took public transportation to high school, museums, the Met, Central Park, and to my first part-time job as a gift wrapper in a shop on 37th Street at Fifth Avenue. As a result I feel more alive in a city. I love its zest and hum.

As Grace and I have explored LA together, I have felt again that stimulation. I love the grand buildings, the parks, and the extensive public art. I love seeing what LA was "back in the day." I love unearthing the history and the stories of the people who have created Los Angeles. At the same time, I have come to know LA on a more human scale as we have journeyed through the neighborhoods on foot and by bus, light rail, and Metrolink. The urban myth that people in big cities are unfriendly was definitely debunked for us. On each of our Adventures we have found the people of LA to be helpful and friendly. LA is one great city!

AUTHORS' PREFACE

Another Book about Los Angeles?

Who needs it? What hasn't already been said about Los Angeles?

LA is glorious, but complex. It is simultaneously blessed with space, good weather, diversity, history, high culture, and a wonderful wackiness where innovation reigns.[1] There will *always* be a need for new ways to explore and rediscover this kaleidoscopic city.[2]

But the freeways, often clogged with traffic, and the vast distances between places can be intimidating. How else can you get to a place you want to see if you don't want to drive, or don't want to add to the traffic or air pollution?

That's where this book comes in. So, who needs it? We are emboldened to say, "*Everybody!*" **By using Metrolink, buses, the subway, light rail, and your own two feet, it is possible to explore and enjoy many places in Los Angeles without a car.**[3]

All of our twenty-four Adventures start at Union Station. They take you out into the many neighborhoods of the city and feature both well-known landmarks and overlooked treasures. We agree with the late newspaper columnist and LA fan, **Jack Smith,** who wrote: "The real charm of cities is not always in their famous places but in the hundreds of unheralded and unpretentious places that people discover and enjoy by themselves."[4] We have experienced every one of our Adventures first-hand, traveling countless miles by public transportation in order to verify their worthiness and accessibility.[5]

---

1) For instance, where else can you find a "Mexicatessen" or a place for a "pastrami burrito"? Are there "Thai tacos" in any other city, or such fine examples of *Googie* architecture?

2) "Kaleidoscopic" was the word used to describe the history of Los Angeles by John and LaRee Caughey in their book *Los Angeles, Biography of a City.* University of California Press,1977, page xiv.

3) Bicycles offer another low carbon way to explore Los Angeles. (Entering the search term "Bicycling in Los Angeles" will return several informative websites.)

4) Jack Smith, *Alive in LaLa Land.* New York: Franklin Watts, 1989, 46.

5) Missing from our Adventures are: Travel Town Railroad Museum, the Getty Center and Getty Villa, the Huntington Library and Gardens, and the Norton Simon Museum. A concerted effort

One of our most important discoveries has been the restorative nature of a number of the venues—places that can uplift and inspire the spirit and leave you with a sense of well-being, for instance, a certain spot in a museum, a vista by the river or at the ocean, a garden, a fountain or outdoor sculpture, the exterior of an innovative building, or a particularly beautiful interior. Of course, some venues will change in coming years, but inspiring spaces in the LA area will endure, we hope, forever.

We have deliberately avoided making this a guide to Los Angeles restaurants, because they are apt to change frequently. However, a few special places are mentioned.

This has been a yearlong project for us. The experience has deepened our friendship and greatly expanded our understanding of what there is to be discovered and relished in this sprawling megalopolis, this magic carpet of lights called Los Angeles. **May it be the same for all of you, our fellow adventurers!**

Grace E. Moremen and Jacqueline Nocella Chase
Claremont, California
February 1, 2015

---

was made to reach them by bus, but, in some cases, the bus stopped too far away from the venue and in others, the route proved to be too difficult or cumbersome. Reluctantly, we say that for these places, a car will be necessary.

INTRODUCTION:
Why LA? Why Here?

Before all else, it was the river. Thousands of years ago, the first human inhabitants of the area that would become Southern California established a village near a majestic river that stretched from the mountains to the sea. The people came to be known as the ***Tongva*** and they called their village ***Yang-na.***[1]

A forewarning of change came to *Yang-na* with the arrival of an expedition of Spanish soldiers on August 2, 1769. Commanded by Gaspar de Portolá, they were on their way north to Monterey Bay to secure Spain's claim to Alta California before the British or the Russians could do so. Portolá's friendly meeting with the villagers of *Yang-na* is believed to have taken place on land that is now Elysian Park.[2] Father Juan Crespi, a Franciscan priest traveling with Portolá, took note that August 2nd was the feast day of Our Lady Queen of the Angels of Porciuncula.[3] So the newly discovered river was named for the feast day, but shortened to ***El Rio de Los Angeles***, or sometimes just ***Porciuncula***.

Twelve years later, on September 4, 1781, the Spanish came again to *Yang-na*. This time it was a group of forty-four people, called *Los Pobladores*, or "the settlers." Recruited in Mexico by order of King Carlos III of Spain, their task was to establish a town, a *pueblo*, on the shores of *El Rio de Los Angeles*. They were of Mexican, African, and Spanish heritage and included two priests, four soldiers, and eleven

---

1) *Yang-na* was located in the vicinity of today's Civic Center. Later, the Spanish named the *Tongva* people "*Gabrieleños*." Another tribe, the *Chumash*, settled farther north around the Santa Barbara area.

2) An historic marker identifies the approximate location of the place where the Broadway Bridge enters Elysian Park.

3) *Porciuncula* means "portion" in Spanish. It refers to a small portion of land near Assisi, Italy, given to St. Francis on which to build a chapel. Called "Our Lady Queen of the Angels," the chapel is decorated with a mural depicting the Annunciation. In Italy, because of its close association with St. Francis, this tiny chapel is greatly revered, it has been contained within a large basilica which was built around it.

families. They broke their journey at Mission San Gabriel[4] before continuing the final eight miles to their destination. It was natural that they would name their tiny outpost on the edge of Spain's colonial empire after the river: ***El Pueblo de Nuestra Señora la Reina de Los Angeles de Porciuncula.*** And so ***Los Angeles*** was born.[5]

4) See Adventure 24 for a visit to the San Gabriel Mission.
5) Information for the Introduction came from *Angel Walk*, City of Los Angeles, 2005, and John and LaRee Caughey, *Los Angeles: Biography of a City*, University of California Press, 1977.

DEMYSTIFYING THE GEOGRAPHY OF LOS ANGELES

Think of the greater metropolitan region of Los Angeles as a square. The Pacific Ocean borders both the left (west) side, site of Santa Monica, and the bottom (south) side, site of Long Beach. The mountains and the San Fernando Valley border the top (north) side, and the San Gabriel Valley borders the right (east) side. The Los Angeles River bisects, more or less, the square from the mountains on the north to the ocean on the south. The square forms the parameters for our **Twenty-Four Adventures,** which cover almost every sector of the LA area.

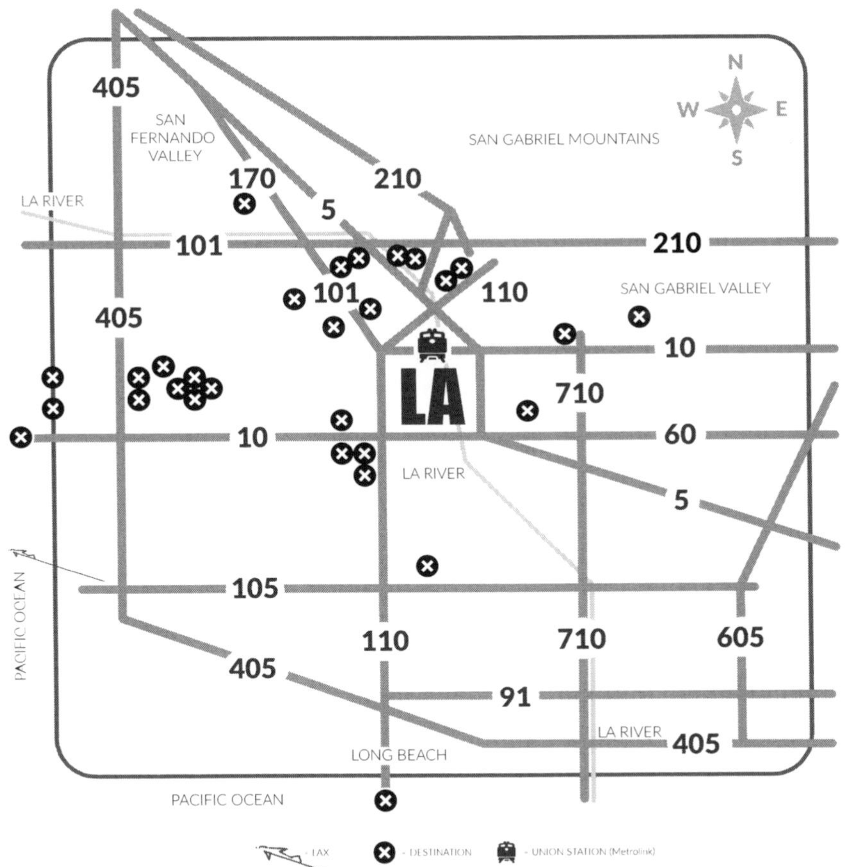

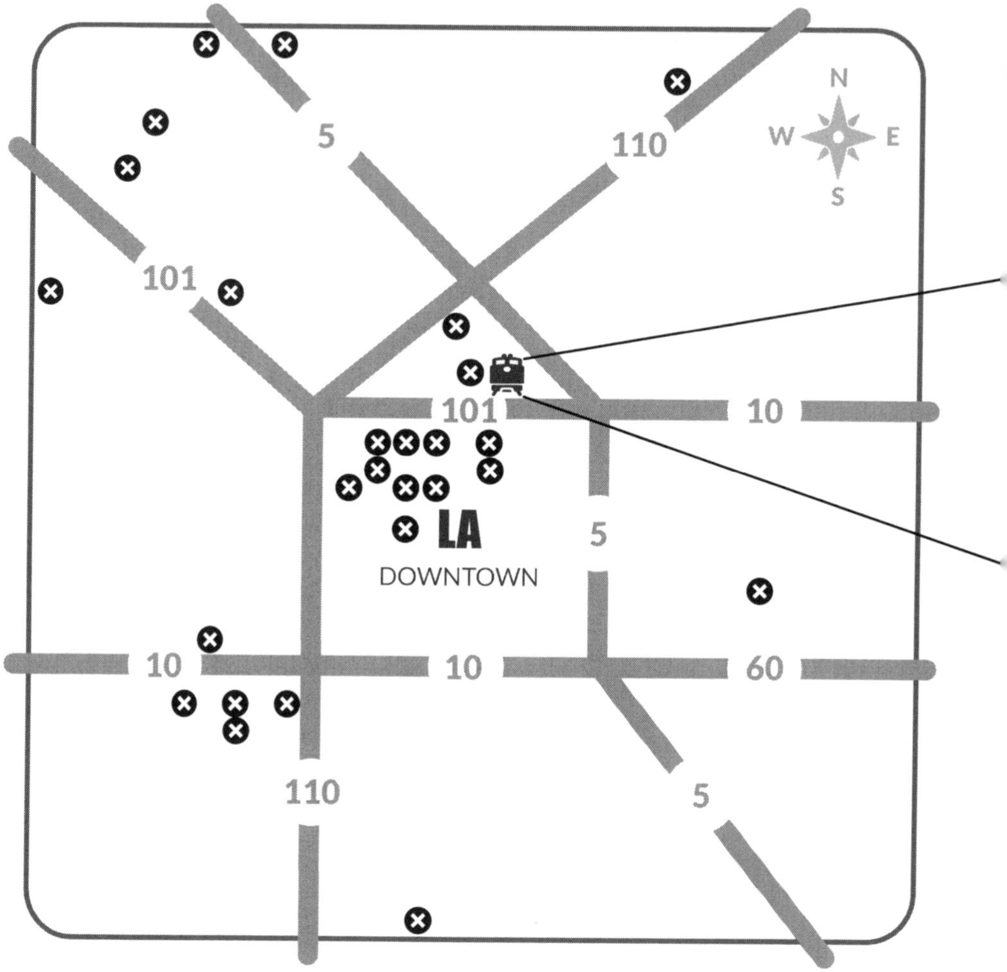

LA

DOWNTOWN

= DESTINATION

= ADVENTURE #

= UNION STATION (Metrolink)

= TIME ESTIMATE

= SUBWAY (Red or Purple Line)

= ADDED COSTS (ESTIMATE)

= LIGHT RAIL (Blue, Expo, Gold, or Green Line)

= BUS (Metro, Dash, or Rapid) = WALKING

Icons courtesy of Flaticon

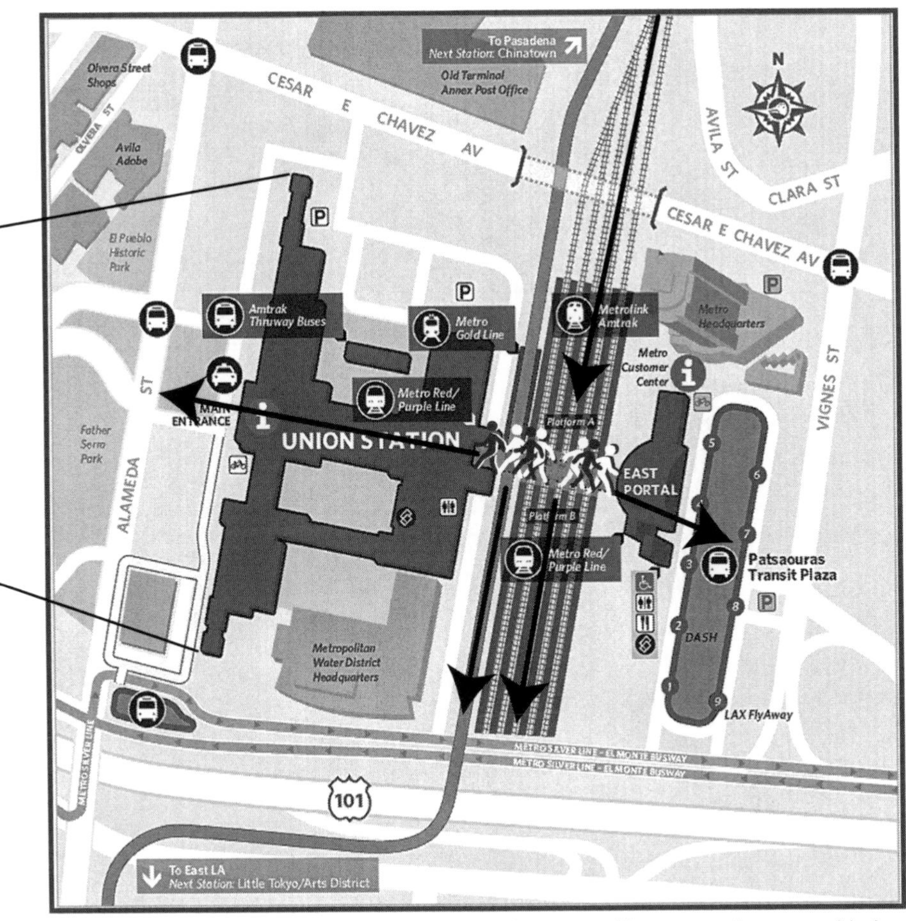

Metrolink website's map of Union Station with arrows of ingress and egress added.

One of two simplified, abstract map graphics (shown on the previous two pages) is used as an inset on the facing page of each of the twenty-four chapters. Destination indications are approximate only, so please consult more accurate maps for more exact locations. In the rest of this book the number of map labels are greatly reduced for the sake of reduced visual clutter. (*Try to name all the freeways from memory; it's a fun test!*) The **Icon Key** at left displays the symbol definitions used throughout, especially on the title page of each chapter. We hope you find them intuitive, clear, and useful.

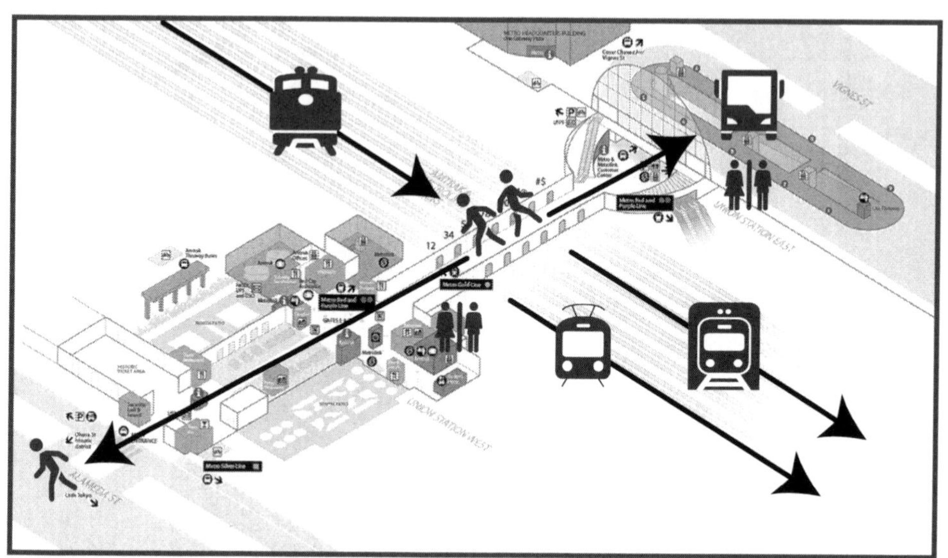

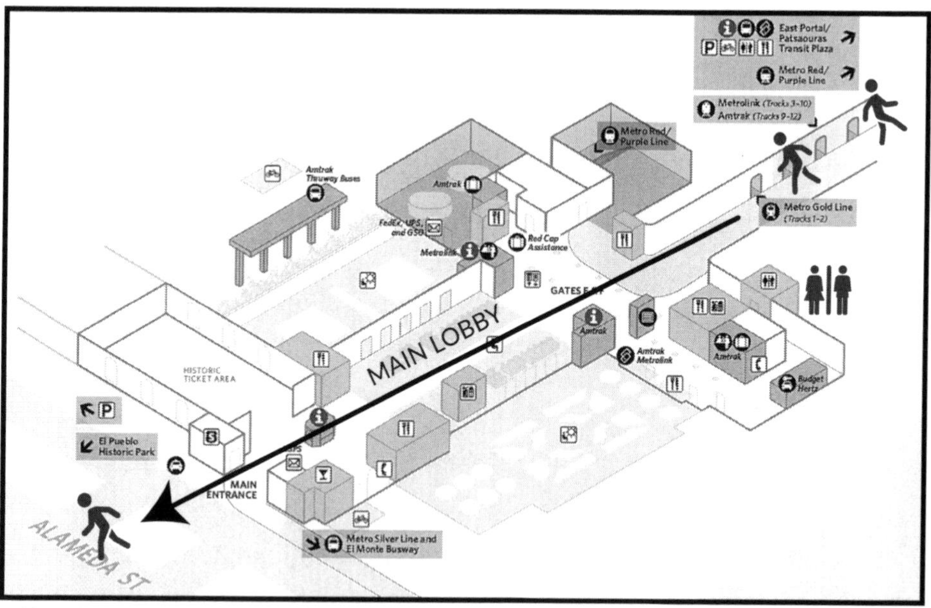

Metrolink website diagrams of Union Station with arrows of arrival and departure added.

All of our Adventures start from **Union Station; the estimated total times include the round trip travel time.** Above, lines of Metrolink (or Amtrak) arrival and various means of departure are indicated. The **Red, Gold, and Purple Lines** each have their own gate.

Walking west through the magnificent main lobby to **Alameda Street,** or the other way through the **East Portal** to the **Patsaouras Transit Plaza**, you will find stops for the various buses.

We do appreciate the irony of indicating freeways—those very things that we are trying to avoid—to orient our map graphics. But since LA is known for its freeways, understanding how they fit into the total picture is paramount. We hope that seeing how the freeways relate geographically to our Adventures will be helpful to our travelers.

Be sure to visit our website, **LovingLA.com**, for larger color versions of these diagrams, plus links to all the websites we mention in the book, color versions of the black and white photos, additional photos, updates, anecdotes, corrections, and **even more Adventures**!

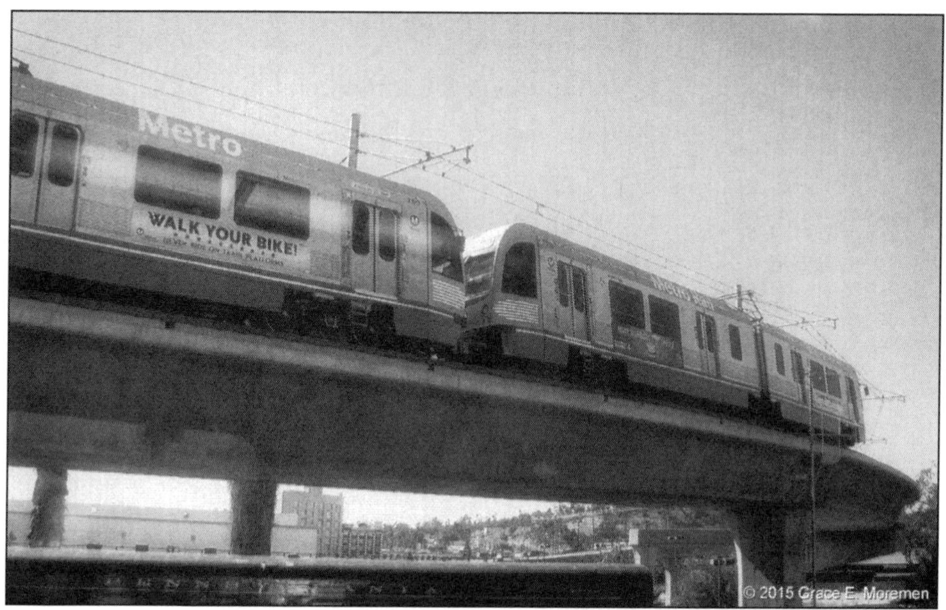
Metro
WALK YOUR BIKE!
© 2015 Grace E. Moremen

© 2015 Grace E. Moremen

CAREFUL, CAR FREE, AND COST CONSCIOUS: IMPORTANT INFORMATION ABOUT TRAVELING IN LOS ANGELES

Safety

Remember to be prudent. You are traveling in a big city. Keep your valuables close to you and stay alert to your surroundings at all times. Traveling in twos or threes is more fun and probably safer than going alone.

About the Buses and Trains

Metrolink

The Metrolink is Southern California's regional passenger rail system. For more information **call 1-800-371-5465** or go to www.metrolinktrains.com

Schedules are available at **Union Station** or on the train.

Purchase your Metrolink round-trip ticket at a machine on the platform of your local station. Your ticket has a bar code **and may be used to transfer to subway, light rail, or bus in Los Angeles.**

When you get to Union Station and want to transfer to subway or light rail, "tap" your ticket at the turnstile. If you want to transfer to a bus, show your ticket to the driver.

If you don't have a Metrolink ticket, you can purchase a **Tap Card**[1] at the **Tap vending machines in Union Station**. Cost is $1.00 for the card, $1.75 for a one-way ride, and $7.00 for a Day Pass. If you are eligible for a reduced-fare Senior Day Pass, you get your card at the information window at the east end of Union Station. **If you need help, find one of the station employees wearing a red jacket. They circulate along the main passageway and at the east end of Union Station.**

1) "Tap" stands for Transit Access Pass.

The Los Angeles County Metropolitan Transit Authority (MTA)

The major transportation provider for the City and County of Los Angeles.

MTA operates four types of service

 (a) (Subway) "Rapid Transit"

Red Line, Purple Line, referred to as **Metro**

 (b) Light Rail "Lines"

Blue, Gold, Green, and Expo Lines

(*The Orange and Silver Lines are bus extensions.*)

 (c) Metro Local (orange) Bus

The most common bus in the city

 (d) Metro Rapid (red) Bus

Many articulated, or extra-long

Metro Rapid Bus (red, articulated)

Metro Local Bus (orange)

If you do not have a Metrolink **Ticket** or a **Tap Card**— the **bus fares are $1.75 regular adult, seniors 75¢ @ peak hours and 35¢ off-peak.** <u>Exact change required</u>.

Off-peak hours are **9:00am–3:00pm** and **7:00pm–5:00am.** Front-mounted bicycle racks (for two bikes only) and lifts to accommodate disabled passengers are on all buses. *Bicycles are a great way to travel carbon free in LA.*

The Dash Bus (LADOT)

The Dash Bus system maintains frequent service for short hops in downtown and twenty-six other neighborhoods; it is free with your Metrolink ticket, otherwise it is 50¢. The Dash buses are operated by the Los Angeles Department of Transportation, LADOT. For information go to **ladottransit.com/dash/**

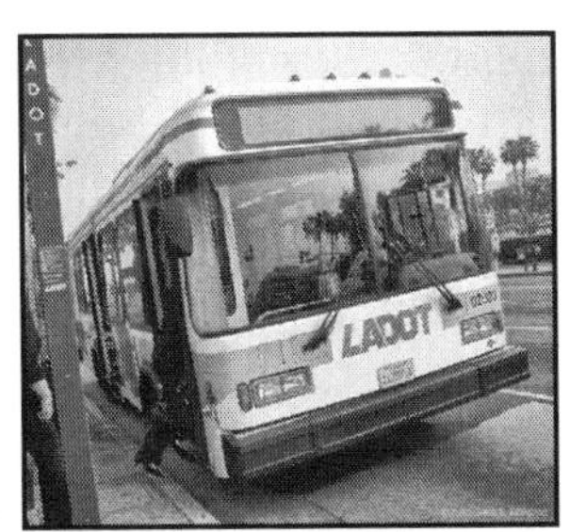

The Big Blue Bus

Photo courtesy AllyUnion ©2008

System provides service to Santa Monica and the west side of Los Angeles. It does ***not*** give you free rides with your Metrolink ticket. Adult fare $1 for local bus, $2 for I-10 Freeway Express. Senior and Disabled 50¢ for local bus, $1 for I-10 Freeway Express. **For information go to their website: bigbluebus.com**

For information about a specific destination:
call 323-466-3876 or go to **www.metro.net**
Hours: Monday–Friday • 6:30am–7:00pm
Saturday & Sunday • 8:00am–4:30pm

For customer relations **call 213-922-6235**
In Union Station there is a **free telephone service** located at the east end of the station. Just pick up the receiver and a **live operator** will answer. Tell the operator your starting point and destination.

Bus schedules are available on racks near the telephone.

Estimating Basic Cost of an Adventure:

Estimates ***do not*** include cost of Metrolink.

Entrance fees and any additional costs for each Adventure are indicated at the start of each chapter in a moneybag icon.

The amount indicated is usually the **total of any adult fees** anticipated. *(Often children, seniors, and students receive a discounted rate.)* **Please keep in mind that the cost indicated should only be viewed as a benchmark to help budget your trip.** It ***does not include*** normal public transportation costs, and usually does not include dining costs—although occasionally a specifically recommended restaurant, bakery, or buffet price is added in.

Note that prices and costs do change, and some listed here almost certainly will. Please check either **LovingLA.com** or vendors' websites for updates, corrections, and the most current pricing information.

The following are our ballpark estimates for typical dining costs:

Bring your own lunch, buy one beverage = about $5
Buy sandwich and beverage = about $15
Restaurant = allow $20–30 *(check prices first!)*

CONTENTS

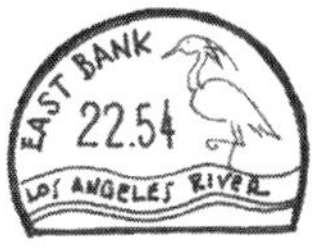
EAST BANK
22.54
LOS ANGELES RIVER

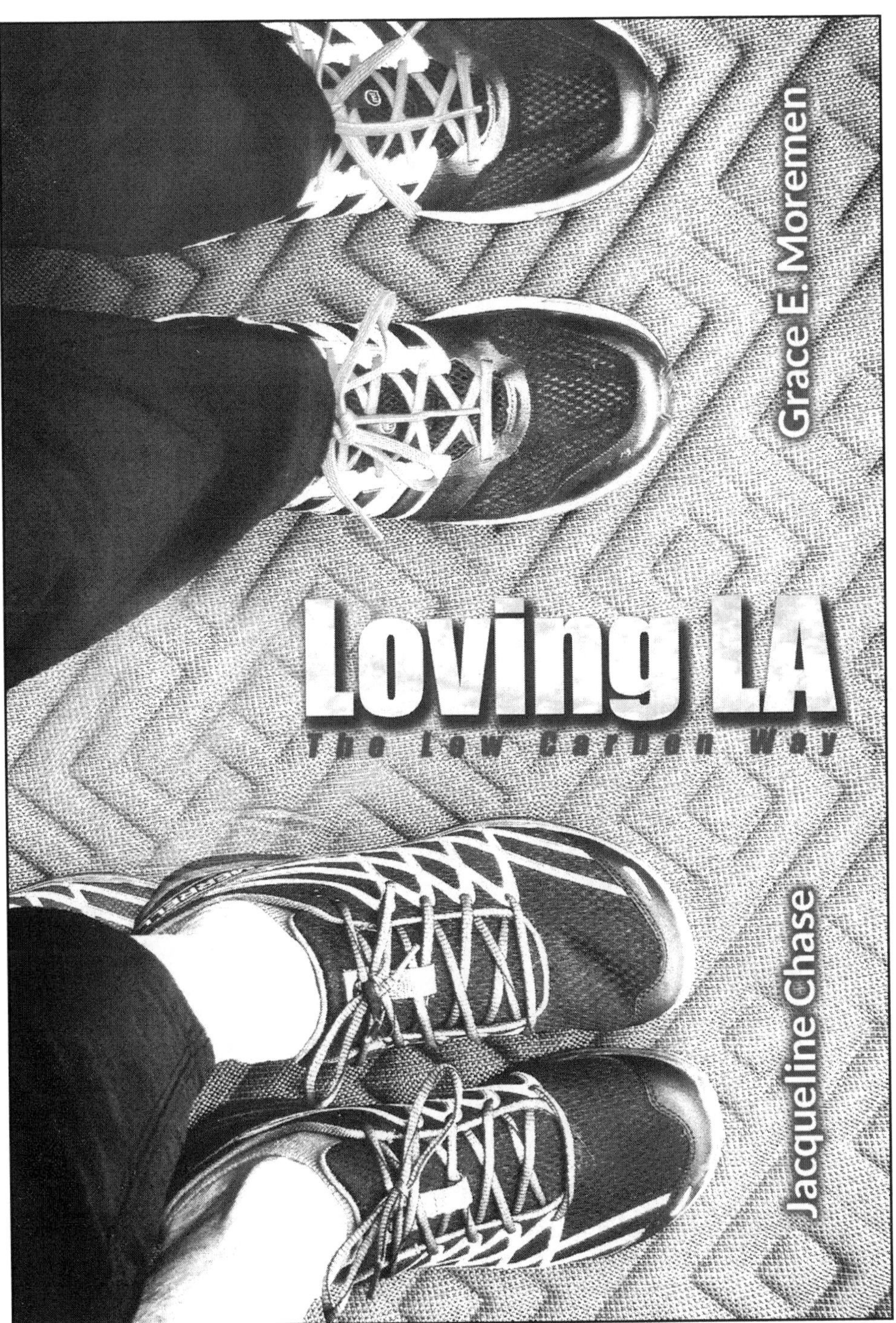
Grace E. Moremen
Loving LA
The Low Carbon Way
Jacqueline Chase

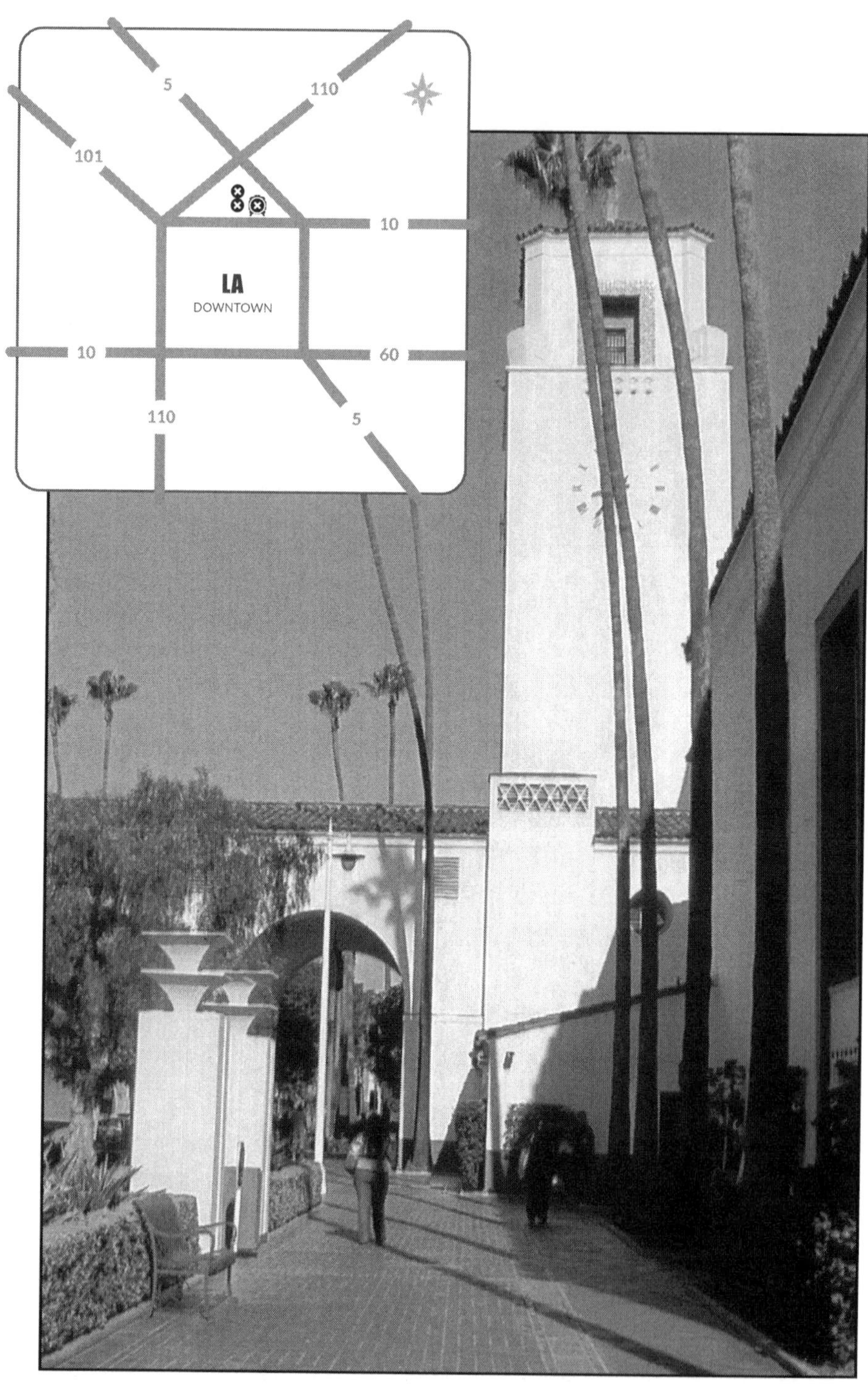
5
110
101
10
LA
DOWNTOWN
10
60
110
5

1

Exploring the Heart of Los Angeles

Union Station • El Pueblo de Los Angeles Historic Monument • Olvera Street

It has been said that Los Angeles has no center, no heart. We disagree! Granted, LA's size and geographical complexities are a challenge. But, as we see it, the city has a heart, a heart with two halves: the historic ***Old Plaza*** *and the modern Union Station, located less than one hundred yards apart. For this Adventure, you need only your feet and a good pair of walking shoes (or a mobility scooter, if required). Begin with elegant Union Station, then cross the street to the Old Plaza and Olvera Street.*

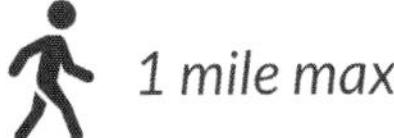

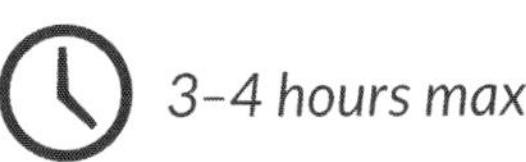

If you are traveling into Los Angeles on Metrolink, shortly before you reach **Union Station** you will see the **Los Angeles River.** You may ask, "Why does it look like a giant drain with only a trickle at the bottom?" The answer is that although Southern California has a long dry season, it can also experience torrential winter rains every ten years or so, and when that happens, the LA River channel stands ready to contain the enormous runoff that cascades down with unbelievable speed from the surrounding mountains.[1]

1) The story of the LA River is complex. It is well explained in the poetic book, *Rio LA: Tales from the Los Angeles River,* by Patt Morrison, with photographs by Mark Lamonica. Angel City Press, 2001.

As your train crosses the river, look south to see the handsome **First Street Bridge** that links **Little Tokyo** to **East LA.** Or, quickly look north for a glimpse of the **Cesar Chavez Bridge,** and beyond that the tree-covered hills of **Elysian Park,**[2] while the hazy-blue **San Gabriels** rise in the distance.

© 2015 Grace E. Moremen

Union Station

800 N. Alameda Street

213-683-6729

Gleaming Union Station[3] awaits you, all spiffed up for its 75th anniversary, celebrated in 2014. Built in 1939, on the eve of World War II, it soon served as a busy center for transporting servicemen and women. But during the postwar years, with the decline of rail travel, Angelenos

2) An area rich in history. See Introduction.

3) Built jointly by the Union Pacific, Southern Pacific, and Santa Fe railroads, the station's design and construction were coordinated by the local architectural firm of John and Donald Parkinson.

almost forgot their railroad station. Things began to change in 1991 with the opening of Metrolink commuter rail, and ridership has grown dramatically as the Metro Light Rail/Subway system has expanded. The Metropolitan Transportation Authority (MTA) bus service, too, has markedly improved since funds were increased in 1996.[4]

If this is your first visit to LA Union Station, you may be overwhelmed by the soaring beauty of the *Mission Revival*-style waiting room that has been likened to the nave of a great cathedral with its high, beamed ceilings, circular chandeliers, tall windows, polished marble floor, and colorful tiles. But also look for the 1930s *Art Deco* details that abound. The place is warm and welcoming, and its two patios, north and south, lure travelers to enjoy the Southern California sunshine.[5]

4) The improved service was the result of The Bus Riders Union winning a class action suit against the MTA. Edward W. Soja, *My Los Angeles*. University of California Press, 2014, 226.
5) The restoration of Union Station during 1996–1999 was led by Ira Yellin, "long time champion" of Los Angeles's historic core. *Los Angeles Times*, September 11, 2002.

To see the opposite end of Union Station, walk east through the pedestrian tunnel to the **East Portal,** a 1996 addition that links the station to the **Patsaouras Transit Plaza,** a hub for buses. The number of art pieces in this part of the station might surprise you. At the escalator entrance to the Metro Red/Purple Line you will see the **electronic mural, *A Train*,** by **Bill Bell,** composed of "light sticks" depicting patterns of cars, buses, trains, and the faces of some celebrities. Installed in 1996, it was one of the first high-tech murals in the United States. Watch it for a while and see if you can decipher the images.

Traveler by Terry Schoonhoven

Take the escalator or the elevator down one flight and you will come upon the engaging **tile mural, *Traveler*,** by **Terry Schoonhoven** (1945–2001), an impression of time travel that beckons you to step back in history. Don't miss the cat whose coat changes color as it jumps from the past into the present. And notice the letter on the ground. Was it put there by the man from the past who is looking out at us, or by an unseen hand from our time who wants the man to pick it up?

1

Back on the main floor, look up at the giant **mural *City of Dreams/ River of History*** by local African American artist **Richard Wyatt.** Then notice **May Sun's *River Bench*** that is capped by a pyramid containing bottles and broken crockery excavated from the site of the first Chinatown when Union Station was built.[6] Take a few minutes to go over to the **Aquarium,** designed by marine biologist **Oscar Weathersby.** Do you see the school of large (appropriately chosen) angelfish?

El Pueblo de Los Angeles Historic Monument

845 N. Alameda Street

213-628-1274

Leave the station by the west doors. Cross Alameda Street and walk up the slope to the **Old Plaza** or **El Pueblo Historic Monument,** the birthplace of Los Angeles. The people wisely moved their town to this site on higher ground after the river overflowed its banks in the wet winter of 1814–15, and their adobe buildings were swept away or ruined.

6) There is a dark side to the story. In order to build on this site, the City Council made the decision to evict the Chinese community that had lived here for generations. Many of the people relocated several blocks northwest and formed a new Chinatown (Adventure 5). A line in the paving of Union Station's south patio, dated 1887, marks the boundary of the original Chinatown.

Four enormous **Moreton Bay fig trees** shade the plaza. Planted in the 1870s, they are over 150 years old. On weekends, the air of the plaza may be filled with the strains of mariachi music or the pulsing beats of a drum to accompany dancers. There is much history in this place to learn and experience. South of the bandstand, take note of **Founders' Plaque,** a memorial to the forty-four hardy souls who, in 1781, became the first residents of Los Angeles (see our Introduction). Their names appear on the plaque and also on medallions embedded in the sidewalk encircling the plaza.

Three gentlemen who were important to the city's beginnings will greet you if you take time to look. Their bronze statues are: on the east, **King Carlos III of Spain** (1716–1788),[7] the reigning monarch who granted approval for the *Pueblo* to be founded on the banks of the *Porciuncula;* on the west, **Philipe de Neve,** (1724–1784),[8] the Spanish governor of California who made the recommendation to the king, and who laid out the first streets of the town; and in a grassy area on the east, the Franciscan monk **Junipero Serra** (1713–1784), founder of the California missions, who raises high the cross of his faith. Records show that de Neve quarreled repeatedly with Father Serra over the secularization of the missions. Perhaps it is fitting that the priest's statue is located on a separate plot of land.[9] Take a close look at **King Carlos.** He will look right back at you with a slightly smiling expression and follow you with his eyes.

The **Old Firehouse** (1834), on the south side, is one of the oldest buildings on the plaza. Now a museum, it displays antique firefighting equipment, a 19th-century firehouse clock, a supersized alarm bell, and vintage photographs.

7) Sculpted by Federico Coullant-Valera, the statue was dedicated by King Juan Carlos I and Queen Sofia of Spain in 1987.
8) Sculpted by Henry Lion, 1932.
9) Father Serra's statue was sculpted by Ettore Cadorin in 1931. Los Angeles was not chosen as a mission site. However, Mission San Gabriel Arcángel was only eight miles to the east (Adventure 24-b).

1

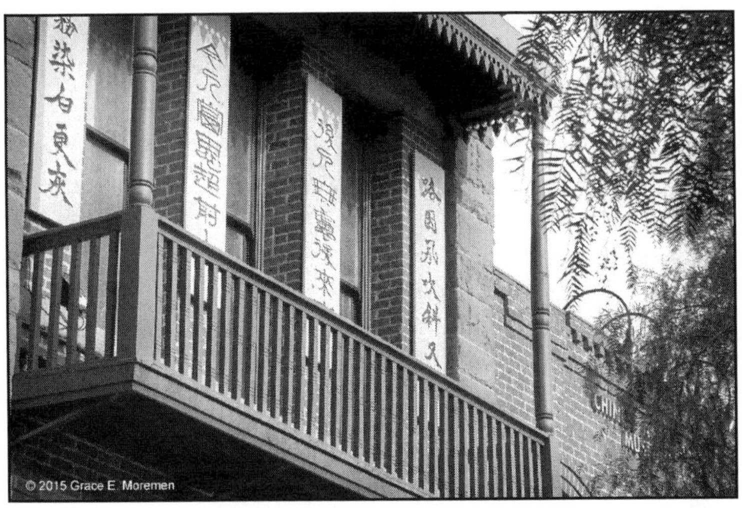

The Garnier Building's balcony

Around the corner on Los Angeles Street, don't miss a remnant of LA's first Chinatown: the **Garnier Building** (1890). It is the sole surviving structure from the days when the Chinese community was located along Los Angeles Street. Notice the balcony where four banners are hanging, reminiscent of old photographs. The Chinese characters on the banners display two poetry couplets, called *dui lian*. Translated, the two inner *dui lian* say: "The previous generation didn't worry about their posterity; nowadays, people should get a step ahead of the previous generation." The outer *dui lian* say: "Due to the wind, there are many twists and turns in the road; due to the mist, color can change from white to gray."[10] Today, this handsome brick building houses the **Chinese-American Museum. Enter on Sanchez Street off the south side of the plaza.** Ground floor exhibits tell the story of Chinese Americans in Los Angeles. Rotating art exhibits fill attractive galleries on the second and third floors.

Hours: Tuesday–Sunday • 10:00am–3:00pm
Closed Mondays and major holidays
Cost: Donations

10) Translation supplied by Sylvia Shen, a native Chinese speaker with a masters' degree in library science from Columbia University, and Angela Donnelly, a Chinese scholar.

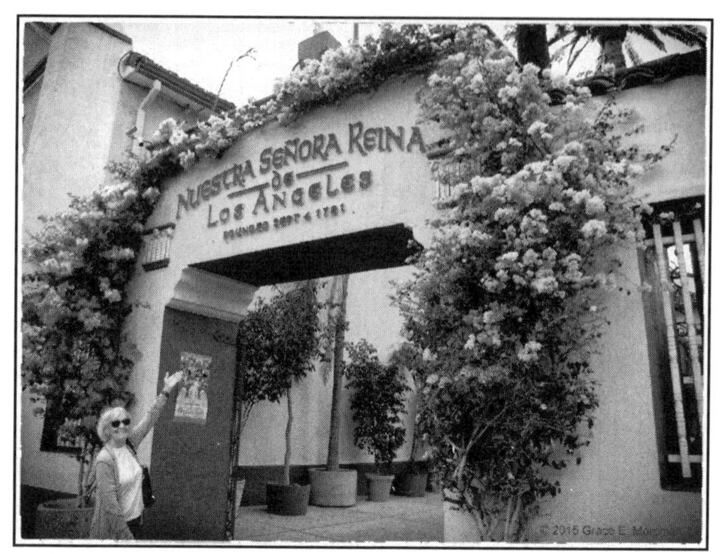

Also on the south side of the plaza is the imposing *Italianate*-style **Pico House** (1870), designed by **Ezra Keysor** (1835–1907).[11] It was built as a hotel by **Pio de Jesus Pico** (1801–1894), the last Mexican governor of California, and was the city's first three-story building. Although not regularly open, the interior is often used for art exhibits at which time it is accessible to the public. The Pico House has a light-filled courtyard, not visible from the street, and a spacious front room with large windows. Next door are the **Merced Theatre,** also designed by Keysor in 1870, and the **Masonic Hall** (1858). These buildings are not currently open to the general public.

On the plaza's west side, on Main Street, is the **Plaza de Cultura y Artes (Museum of Mexican-American Culture).** Opened in 2011 in historic buildings, this welcoming museum has nicely arranged displays that clarify and celebrate Mexican American history and culture in Los Angeles and California.

Hours: 12:00am–7:00pm

Closed Tuesdays and holidays

Admission is free

11) Ezra Keysor also designed St. Vibiana's, the former cathedral, at Main and Second streets (Adventure 6).

1

At the northwest corner of the plaza you will find a little church, affectionately called ***La Placita.*** It was built between 1818 and 1822, soon after the *Pueblo* relocated to higher ground. Offically known as ***La Iglesia de Nuestra Senora La Reina de Los Angeles de Porciuncula,*** it is much loved, especially by the Latino community, and is the location of choice for the baptism of children.[12] The church has been remodeled several times over the years. On the outside wall of the north side of the church is a large mural of **Our Lady of Guadalupe.**

Free walking tours of the plaza are given Tuesday through Saturday at 10:00am, 11:00am, and noon. Meet in front of the Tour Office (green awning) next to the Old Firehouse. **Call 213-628-1274 for information. Reservations are suggested for parties larger than six.**

Now head over to **Olvera Street** on the north side of the plaza. Established in 1930 as a re-creation of a Mexican marketplace, this street remains perennially popular. It takes its name from the first Superior Court Judge in Los Angeles, **Augustin Olvera** (1818–1876), whose house once stood at the entrance to the street (now the site of the Plaza Methodist Church).[13]

Originally, what is now "Olvera Street" was nothing more than an alley that ran between houses facing east toward Alameda Street and west toward Main Street. The first houses built along the alley were adobes. Remarkably, one of those adobes still stands. Built in 1818 by Don Francisco Jesus de Avila soon after the town moved to higher ground, the **Avila Adobe** is the oldest house in Los Angeles. But it almost did not survive. After Avila died in 1832 and the house changed hands, gradually, over time it deteriorated, and so did the alley. By the late 1920s, the adobe was scheduled for demolition. It was rescued through the fund-raising efforts of a philanthropist

12) The mural on the front of the church, *The Annunciation,* is a copy by **Isabel Piczek** of the central panel on the chapel near Assisi by **Ibario da Viterbo.** The name of that chapel is Our Lady Queen of the Angels of Porciuncula. Grace finds it fascinating that from this tiny chapel in Italy came the name for a great city, with a population of 16.4 million in the wider metropolitan area as of the year 2000.

13) The Plaza Methodist Church maintains an extensive museum of local history.

Olvera Street

125 Paseo de la Plaza
213-628-1274

named **Christine Sterling** (1881–1963).[14] The alley's transformation into a colorful marketplace came about in order to provide an attractive setting for the restored adobe. Today the Avila Adobe is owned by the City of Los Angeles. It has been charmingly furnished as the home of a well-to-do *Californio* of the 1840s.

Hours: Open daily 9:00am–4:00pm,
except Thanksgiving and Christmas
Admission is free

Other historical buildings also occupy Olvera Street. Midway along the street stands the **Sepulveda House** (1887). Designed by noted British architect **Charles Eastlake** (1836–1906), this attractive

14) Christine Sterling is honored by a large photo and plaque inside the entrance to the Old Winery. She is also credited with developing Olvera Street as a Mexican marketplace.

Victorian brick structure fronts on North Main Street. It started life as a boarding house, but is now the **Visitors' Information Center.** A couple of rooms have been set aside as a museum. Another historic dwelling is the **Pelanconi House** (1855–57); it is occupied by La Golondrina Restaurant, a longtime tenant.[15] Across the way is another old-timer, El Paseo Restaurant. Both serve delicious Mexican food and have pleasant outdoor eating areas.

Not to be missed on Olvera Street is the 1932 **mural, *Tropical America,***[16] by acclaimed Mexican artist **David Alfaro Siqueiros** (1896–1974).[17] **The Interpretive Center** explains the background of this work through excellent displays. Painted on an outside wall of a building on Olvera Street, the mural's central figure is a crucified Mexican peasant with an American eagle overhead. The radical political subject matter so shocked Angelenos in 1932 that it was soon whitewashed over. For decades it remained hidden. But after forty years of exposure to the weather, Siqueiros's images slowly began to reappear, like ghosts from the past.[18] In 1977, painstaking work began to conserve it. Finally put on view in 2012, the mural is still rather faint but can be perceived. Its presence has had a profound effect on the Chicano muralist movement in Los Angeles. It can be observed from a platform above the Interpretive Center.

Hours: Tuesday–Sunday • 10:00am–3:00pm

Closed Mondays and holidays

Admission is free

As you leave Olvera Street and head back to Union Station, look to your left and delight in another mural, the captivating ***Blessing of the Animals*** (1974–1978) by **Leo Politi** (1908–1996),[19] on the wall of the

15) Grace remembers eating there as a child. It was one of the few Mexican restaurants in Los Angeles in the 1930s and 1940s that catered to Anglos.

16) Its full title is *Tropical America: Oppressed and Destroyed by Imperialism*.

17) Siqueiros was a contemporary of Mexican artists Diego Rivera and Jose Clemente Orozco.

18) Art historian Isabel Rojas Williams, Claremont, November 18, 2014.

19) Leo Politi (1908–1996) was a local artist and author, most noted for his children's books about life in Los Angeles. Another of his murals decorates a wall at Castelar Elementary School in LA's Chinatown (Adventure 5).

Biscaluz Building. It honors the ceremony held at Olvera Street every Saturday before Easter since 1938. Don't miss the mini portrait of two dogs playing that appears at the bottom of the mural.

Just beyond that you will see **La Placita de Dolores,** a small plaza dominated by an equestrian statue of Mexican singer and movie actor **Antonio Aguilar** (1919–2007). Known as the "Mexican Singing Cowboy," Aguilar was the first Mexican performer to have a star on Hollywood Boulevard's *Walk of Fame.* The statue was dedicated in 2012.

President Jimmy Carter opened La Placita de Dolores on Cinco de Mayo, 1979. It commemorates Mexico's struggle to become independent from Spain. You will see a replica of the **Bell of Dolores** rung in 1810 in the town of Dolores by the priest **Miguel Hidalgo** (1753–1811). Called the father of Mexico's independence, Hidalgo led an uprising of indigenous people to protest the injustices of Spanish rule. The event is illustrated at the far end of the placita in a mural by Mexican-American artist and former UC professor **Eduardo Carrillo** (1937–1997) entitled ***Father Hidalgo Rang the Bell of Dolores.*** Painted on dark blue tile, it portrays the courage of the *campesinos* as they carry the banner of Our Lady of Guadalupe in the face of Spain's powerful soldiers on horseback. The mural is a reminder that the City of the Angels also belonged to Spain at that time and underscores the Spanish/Mexican heritage that lives on in the historic heart of Los Angeles.

❶

Bell of Dolores (replica) rung by Father Hidalgo in 1810

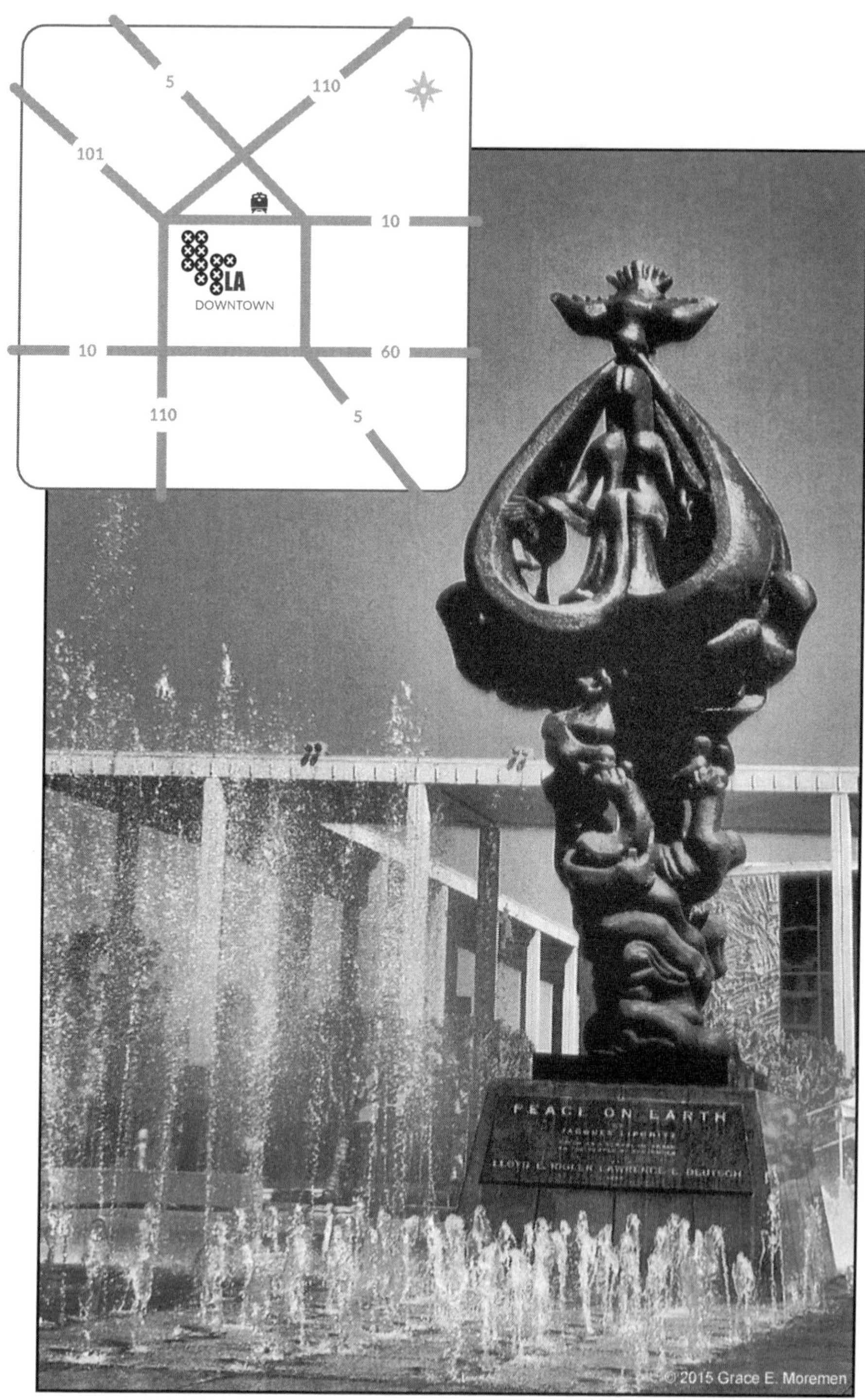
5
110
101
10
LA
DOWNTOWN
10
60
110
5
PEACE ON EARTH
© 2015 Grace E. Moremen

Bunker Hill and Beyond

The Music Center • Mark Taper Forum • Ahmanson Theater • Walt Disney Concert Hall • Red Cat • The Broad Museum • Museum of Contemporary Art (MOCA) • Angels Flight • Grand Central Market • Bradbury Building • Bridget (Biddy) Mason Park • The Last Bookstore

This adventure is ambitious. But if you are willing, it will introduce you to a cluster of precious sites in downtown Los Angeles, some famous, others barely known. Use your discretion regarding length of stay at each venue. ***Be sure to wear comfortable walking shoes and get an early start.****

 *2½ miles max*  *4 hrs minimum* 

MOCA

Your first destination is Bunker Hill, about a mile and a half southwest of Union Station. Take the Metro Red or Purple Line (tap your Metrolink ticket) and get off at the first stop, **Civic Center Station. Exit at First Street. Walk west on First Street two blocks up the hill to Grand Avenue.**

Or, if it's a weekday, take the Dash Bus #B on Alameda Street, directly across from Union Station. The Dash bus is also free with your Metrolink ticket. **Get off at Grand Avenue and First Street.**

* We are indebted to Robert D. Herman for the structure of this Adventure and to his book, *Downtown Los Angeles: A Walking Guide*, 2003.

The Music Center:

Free guided tours of the Music Center

Tuesday–Saturday: 10:30am and 12:30pm

The Dorothy Chandler Pavilion

135 N. Grand Avenue

213-972-0711

Mark Taper Forum

601 W. Temple Street

213-628-2772

Ahmanson Theater

601 W. Temple Street

213-626-2772

The **Disney Hall** is at left, the **Dorothy Chandler Pavilion** and two other theaters are on the right. Together these four theaters make up the **Music Center.** Start with the theaters on your right.

Walk up the steps to the plaza[1] and watch the fountain go through its dramatic cycle. The fountain's central sculpture, ***Peace On Earth***, is by French American artist, **Jacques Lipschitz** (1891–1973). The sculpture, made of black stone, looks dark and forbidding. Perhaps the artist is showing that on earth peace can only be achieved through sacrifice and suffering.

The Dorothy Chandler Pavilion was designed by Welton Beckett & Associates. It opened in 1969 and was heralded as the beginning of a new chapter in the cultural life of Los Angeles. With a seating capacity of 3,197, it is the largest theater at the Music Center. Crystal chandeliers and broad, luxuriously carpeted stairs make it an elegant venue for hosting the LA Opera season and performances of ballet and modern dance. Dorothy Chandler was an active patron of the arts, and the widow of former *LA Times* publisher, Harry B. Chandler.

The second theater in the complex is the **Mark Taper Forum,** named for LA real estate developer and philanthropist S. Mark Taper. Smallest of the theaters, it is built in the round and used for stage plays. Just beyond is the **Ahmanson Theater,** named for philanthropist Howard F. Ahmanson, where large musical productions are staged.

Restrooms on the east side of the plaza at the top of a ramp.

The Walt Disney Concert Hall is the Music Center's fourth venue. It stands on the southwest corner of Grand and First. Initial funding was provided by **Lillian Disney** (1899–1892), widow of the famed moviemaker. Designed by Los Angeles architect **Frank O. Gehry**, it opened in 2003. The innovative *Deconstructivist* style stands out with its convoluted series of stainless steel "petals."[2] Disney Hall is home to the Los Angeles Philharmonic. Many other groups perform here as well, including the Los Angeles Master Chorale. The hall seats 2,265, and is noted for its excellent acoustics. Don't miss the opportunity to go up the outside staircase and see the lovely roof garden—a welcome place for a snack or picnic.

1) An elevator is also available, located on Grand Avenue, a short distance north of First Street.
2) Gehry is world renowned. He designed a beautiful building, similar to the Disney Hall, in Bilbao, Spain (1997), that houses the Guggenheim Museum.

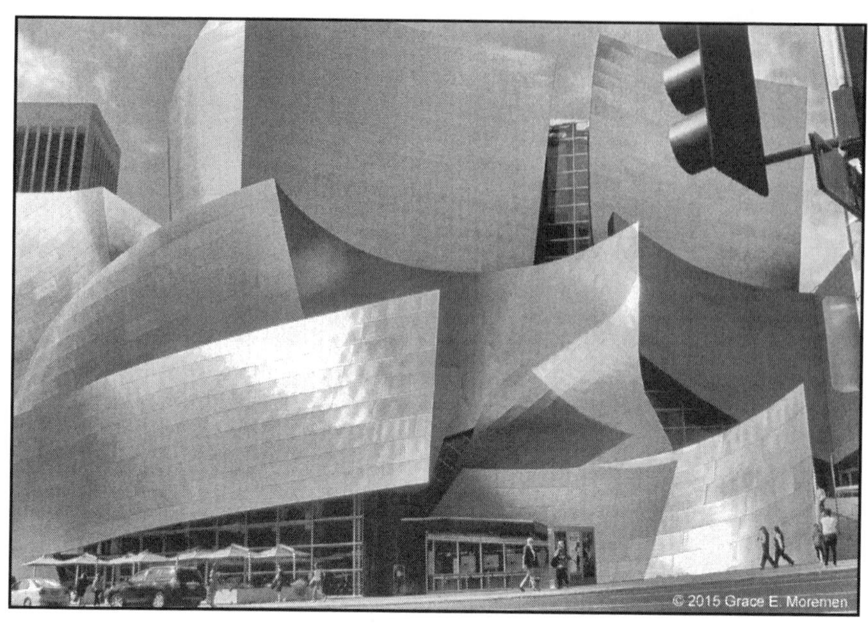

Walt Disney Concert Hall

601 W. Temple Street

213-626-2772

Red Cat
The Roy & Edna Disney Arts Theater

631 W. Second Street (one block west of Grand Avenue)

213-237-2800

All tours begin in the lobby of the Disney Hall. **Call 213-972-4399 for tour information and 213-972-7211 for general information.** You can also take a **self-guided tour of the Disney Hall**; inquire in the lobby. **Restrooms** are located on several levels.

One block west of the Disney Concert Hall, down the hill **on the corner of Second and Hope Streets, is "Red Cat," the Roy and Edna Disney Arts Theater and Gallery,** dedicated to cutting-edge art and dance. **Call 213-972-7211 for information.**

2

The Broad Museum

221 S. Grand Ave

Due to open in late 2015 • thebroad.org

MOCA
Museum of Contemporary Art

250 South Grand Avenue

Monday and Friday: 11:00am–5:00pm

Thursday: 11:00am–8:00pm

Saturday and Sunday: 11:00am–6:00pm.

General Admission: $12

Seniors and Students: $7 • Children ages 0-14: Free

Closed Tuesday and Wednesday

At the **corner of Grand and Second** is the newest addition to Bunker Hill: the **Broad Art Museum.** An exciting three-story structure designed by the New York firm Diller, Scofidio & Renfro, the exterior resembles an enormous honeycomb, while the interior appears undulating and flowing—a fitting environment for Eli Broad's contemporary art collection that numbers over 2,000 works. Scheduled to open in September 2015. **Free admission.**

Cross Grand Avenue at the traffic light and walk south. You pass the **Colburn School of Music Dance and Drama.** Founded in 1950, it moved to its current site in 1998. Go to colburnschool.edu for information. Just next door is the **Museum of Contemporary Art (MOCA),** built in 1986, where works created since 1940 are displayed: *Abstract Expressionist, Pop* to *Postmodern*. Designed by Japanese architect **Arata Isozaki**, the building is striking with its façade of red sandstone and pyramid-shaped skylights.

Continue south to **California Plaza on your left.** Take the steps down to view the fountains and enjoy a **beverage or snack.** There is a **Restroom** at Starbucks.

MOCA Courtyard with *Airplane Parts by* Nancy Rubens (2002)

The entrance to **Angels Flight** (a Los Angeles Cultural-Historical Monument) is at the **east side of the plaza, up the stairs**. Built in 1901 as "The World's Shortest Railway" and reinstalled in 1996, this little funicular narrow gauge railway is a quaint survivor from a simpler age. One of the cars, "Sinai" or "Olivet" (named for biblical mountains), will transport you, for a nominal fee, down the hill. If Angels Flight is closed, **walk down the steps to Hill Street**.

Across the street is the **Grand Central Market**, a neighborhood fixture since 1917, although the building, **designed by John Parkinson**, dates from 1897. A full city block deep, the market extends from Hill Street to Broadway. Fifty-two stalls offer a variety of ethnic foods and take-out meals, and a few upscale food stalls have recently opened as well. It is famous for its fresh produce at reasonable prices.

Walk through the market to Broadway, turn left and go half a block to Third Street. Cross Broadway and you will see the **Bradbury Building on the corner**. It is a National Historic Landmark, **admission is free**. Built in 1893, it was commissioned by

2

Angels Flight

Operates between Hill Street and California Plaza (Bunker Hill)

Cost: 50¢

Grand Central Market

317 S. Broadway

213-624-2378

Bradbury Building

304 S. Broadway

213-626-1893

Lewis Bradbury (1823–1892), a gold mining millionaire. **Designed by George Herbert Wyman (1860–1938),** a young draftsman at the time, the building is his only recognized achievement. But the result is a masterpiece. The Bradbury Building's plain exterior gives no hint of its glorious interior. Seeing it for the first time can be quite overwhelming. It has appeared in several films, including *Blade Runner.*

Bridget (Biddy) Mason Park

S. Broadway and Spring Street • between 3rd & 4th Street

Proceed through the lobby, but stay in the building. Turn right, go up a few stairs, and exit. Now prepare for another surprise. Walk down the steps into **Biddy Mason Park,** tucked in between Broadway and Spring Streets. Created in 1991, this quiet space commemorates **Bridget (Biddy) Mason** (1818–1891), an African American woman who was born a slave in the South. With her master, she came to California in 1856. As California was a free state, a brave and determined Ms. Mason petitioned the court and won her freedom. Trained as a nurse and midwife, Biddy Mason supported herself, purchased land, and built a house near this site. The first African Methodist Episcopal (AME) church in Los Angeles was founded in her living room, and she also established an orphanage. Her portrait and a timeline of her life are displayed on a wall in the park.

2

The Last Bookstore

453 S. Spring Street at 5th Street

213-488-0599 • lastbookstorela.com

Jacqueline having fun with *The Labyrinth of Books. (upstairs)*

Walk to your left through the arcade to Spring Street. There is a café in the arcade in case you would like coffee and/or need a **Restroom. Turn right on Spring Street, and walk to Fifth Street.** On the corner is the **Last Bookstore** (entrance on Fifth), a bibliophile's dream for used and new books. Housed in a former bank building, it is enormous. Go in and take time for a unique LA experience! On the 2nd floor is an installation called "The Labyrinth of Books," plus art stalls with vintage memorabilia and much more. The Last Bookstore is a definite must-see.

Continue west on Fifth for two blocks to Hill Street.

The Pershing Square Metro Station is just ahead for your ride back to **Union Station**. If you **don't have a Metrolink ticket**, the one way ride is $1.75.

5
110
101
10
LA
DOWNTOWN
10
60
110
5

Two Iconic Structures

LA City Hall & The Cathedral of Our Lady of the Angels

This adventure is an architectural delight! You will visit two very different but unforgettable buildings, and have a stroll through ***Grand Park****. And if you go to the* ***Observation Deck of City Hall****, ever afterward, when you look up at the columns just below the pyramid, you will remember being there and seeing the downtown area from that great height. A surprise awaits you on the third floor—****a little-known mini-museum****.*

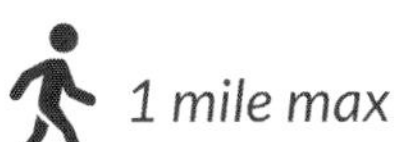

The City Hall of Los Angeles, housing the office of the mayor and the chambers of the City Council, is the center of government in the second largest city in the United States. Built in 1928, it is recognizable around the world, and was the tallest structure in LA until 1964. Architects **John Parkinson, Albert C. Martin**, and **John C. Austin** designed the building in an eclectic style called *Modern American*. The grand courtyard facing Spring Street is *Italianate* in style with classical Corinthian columns—a symbol of civic openness. The building, rising, stately and majestic to twenty-seven stories, incorporates *Art Deco* motifs, and is crowned by an astonishing pyramid in a style borrowed from a tomb built by the ancient Greeks.* The total package is unique, very photogenic, and popular with cinema and television production companies.

*Unless otherwise indicated, major sources for Adventure 3 are the following: *Iconic Vision: John Parkinson, Architect of Los Angeles*, by Stephen Gee (2013); *Angel Walk*, City of Los Angeles, Office of Cultural Affairs (2005); *Los Angeles: An Architectural Guide* by Gebhard and Winter (2003).

Three Optional Routes

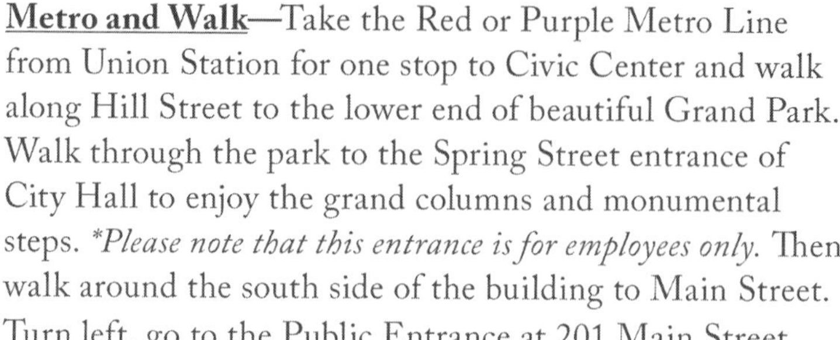

Metro and Walk—Take the Red or Purple Metro Line from Union Station for one stop to Civic Center and walk along Hill Street to the lower end of beautiful Grand Park. Walk through the park to the Spring Street entrance of City Hall to enjoy the grand columns and monumental steps. **Please note that this entrance is for employees only.* Then walk around the south side of the building to Main Street. Turn left, go to the Public Entrance at 201 Main Street.

Walk Only—Walk from Union Station through the Old Plaza and turn left on Main Street crossing over Highway 101 and the Hollywood Freeway to Temple Street. Turn right and walk one block to Spring Street; turn left on Spring and continue to the grand entrance to City Hall, on your left. After viewing the Spring Street entrance, walk around the south side of the building, turn left onto Main Street to the Public Entrance at 201 Main Street.

Longer Walk—Visit the Cathedral of Our Lady of the Angels first. Then walk south on Grand Avenue to the entrance to **Grand Park** which is opposite the Music Center. (This art and music area is discussed in Adventure 2.) Turn into the Park and walk its full length to the Spring Street entrance of City Hall.

Grand Park forms the heart of the Civic Center of Los Angeles. At twelve acres it is one of the largest parks in the downtown area, and its four-block setting spans the distance from the Music Center to LA City Hall. In the park among the spacious and inviting lawns and sitting areas is the **Arthur J. Will Memorial Fountain.**[1] Grand Park also contains a small, intimate performance lawn, a grand event lawn, and terraces planted with drought-tolerant plants—an inviting, garden-filled park for all Angelenos.

---

1) Arthur J. Will was the chief administrative officer of the County of Los Angeles from 1951–1957. It was his vision that Grand Park be a link between the Music Center and City Hall. Recently, the park and fountain have undergone a $56 million makeover with spectacular results.

3

Los Angeles City Hall

200 North Spring Street

Hours: Monday–Friday • 8:00am–5:00pm

Note: Observation Deck is free and open to the public

Once you enter **City Hall**, you go through a security check. Let them know that you want to visit the **Observation Deck**. You will need to show official government identification, such as a driver's license. You will be given a visitor's pass and directions to the Observation Deck.

Take the express elevator to the 22nd floor, transfer to the elevator for the upper floors and take the elevator to the 26th floor, then walk up the stairs to the **Tom Bradley Room** on the Observation level on the 27th floor, or take a second elevator to the 27th floor. The Tom Bradley Room is an open, spacious reception area used for conferences and meetings, adjacent to the Observation Deck.[2]

Walk around the Observation Deck for spectacular 360-degree, unobstructed views of the city, which include Union Station, **Disney Concert Hall**, the **Dragon Gate** to Chinatown and more. At each direction, information is given on what you are viewing. The downtown of Los Angeles is spread before you. When viewing City Hall from the street level, the 27th floor is recognizable by its majestic ring of tall columns that surround the building.

On the way down, stop at the 3rd Floor for a **Restroom,** and to view the beauty of the **Rotunda,** which was the original entrance to LA City Hall until September 11, 2001. Marble floors and columns decorate the chamber. The chandelier was hidden away in boxes after the severe 1933 Long Beach earthquake, and was only reassembled and installed during the 1991 renovations. And also on the third floor is the surprising mini-museum that includes artifacts from Japan and

2) Tom Bradley (1917–1998) was the first African American mayor of Los Angeles, in office from 1973–1993.

View of **Union Station** from the Observation Deck on top of Los Angeles City Hall.

Korea along with the **Los Angeles 1984 Olympic Torch, an original 1928 Wilshire Boulevard streetlight**[3], and the **Los Angeles Flag** that was aboard the seven-crew Space Shuttle Challenger on October 5–13, 1984, notable as being the first crew to include women: **Sally Ride** (1951–2012) and **Kathryn Sullivan** (1951–).

The museum also includes artifacts from Los Angeles's sister city, Nagoya, Japan: the **Mikoshi**, a miniature replica of a Shinto deity's shrine, given in 1963; a **clock,** celebrating the 35th anniversary of the sister cities' relationship; and the **Kasuhisa Replica** model of a festival float used in the Nagoya Matsuri's October festival. The red-haired puppet represents the devil and the black-haired puppet represents an angel. Another Asian country, Korea, is also represented in the museum by a model of the **Turtle Ship** presented by **the mayor of Pusan, Choi Jong Ho,** to commemorate the centennial of U.S.-Korea diplomatic relations. Mexico has a presence in the museum as well with statues of **Benito Juarez** and his wife, **Margarita,**[4] that were presented to Mayor Tom Bradley by the **president of Mexico, Luis Echiverría,** in 1974.

Upon leaving the building **turn left on Main Street and walk north to Temple Street. The Dash Bus "D" to the Cathedral of Our Lady**

3) The streetlight comes from "The day they lined all of Wilshire Boulevard, from downtown LA to the city's 1928 limit at Fairfax Avenue." (Private communication from Eric Lynxwiler, co-author of *Wilshire Boulevard: Grand Concourse of Los Angeles*," Angel City Press, 2011.)

4) Benito Juarez (1806–1872) President of Mexico from 1858–1864, and again from 1867–1872. He was a political reformer who helped to modernize Mexico. His wife was Margarita Maza Perada (1826–1871).

3

Cathedral of Our Lady of the Angels

555 W. Temple Street
Los Angeles, CA 90012
213-680-5200
olacathedral.org
Cathedral tours are free and given
Mondays, Tuesdays, Thursdays, & Fridays: 1:00pm
Wednesdays: 1:15pm
Meet at the lower plaza near the fountain.
Organ recitals and demonstrations of the organ are free:
Wednesdays at 12:45pm

of the Angels stops on the northeast corner of Temple and Main, and runs every five minutes during the day. **Exit at Temple and Hill.**

The Pritzker Prize-winning Spanish architect, **Rafael Moneo,** designed the **Cathedral of our Lady of the Angels**. Architectural styles are *Deconstructivism, Postmodern, Modern,* and *Contemporary*. This glorious cathedral is the seat of the Archdiocese of Los Angeles that serves over five million Catholics. For the faithful, a daily Mass Schedule and the Sacraments of Reconciliation, Baptisms, Weddings and Funerals are offered. Here the archbishop celebrates the major liturgies of the year, along with clergy and laity.

From the outside, the Cathedral looks a bit austere, with its asymmetric architecture and 120-foot bell tower. But when you enter the gate, a welcoming space opens out before you. The golden "sandstone" color of the walls, the arcades, broad plaza and fountain evoke images of the early missions of California.[5] The setting lends itself to liturgi-

5) The unusual looking building with a circular ramp visible across the freeway, to the right of the cathedral, is the Ramon C. Cortines [High] School of Visual and Performing Arts, completed in 2008. It is said that the campus buildings remind the students of themselves, gangly, dreamy, beautiful, and being a bit of an outcast exhibiting strangeness and individuality (central-lausd-ca.schoolloop.com/randarc).

cal, civic, and cultural events but can also be a place of contemplation. Across the plaza from the Cathedral is a **Café** that has outside seating with umbrellas, tables and chairs, and is picnic friendly. Next door is the Cathedral Plaza **Gift Shop** that offers inspirational and religious items for sale. **Restrooms** are located here as well.

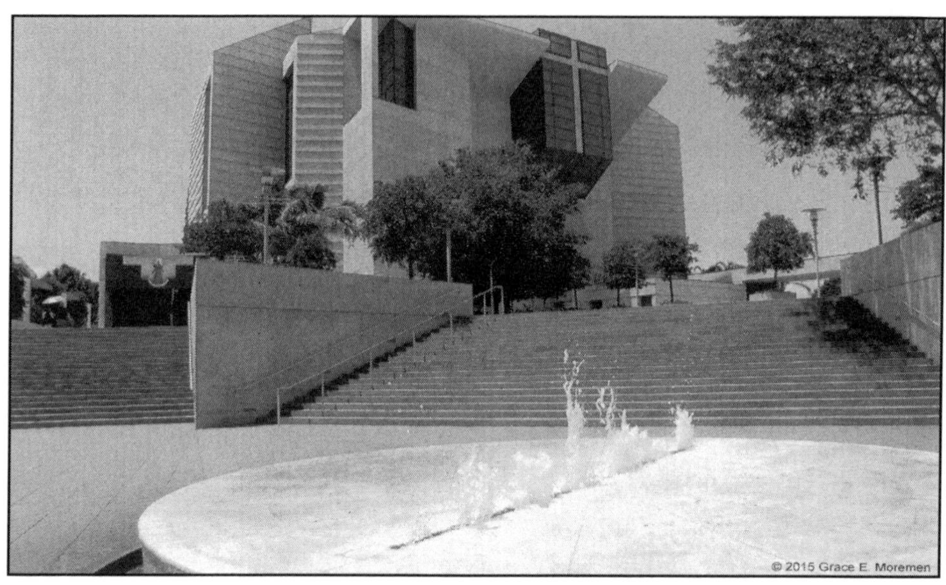

View from the fountain looking up at Our Lady of the Angels Cathedral

As one approaches the bronze doors to enter the Cathedral, look up and see the statue of the Cathedral's namesake, *The Virgin Mary*, designed by **Robert Graham**. As you enter into the vastness of the sanctuary, illuminated by sunlight filtered through windows made of sheets of alabaster, you are in one of the most mystical, uplifting spaces in Los Angeles.[6] At the same time, the atmosphere is warm and inviting.

On the walls are the cathedral's signature fresco-like tapestries, created by artist **John Nava**, that capture both the ancient and the

[6] Julius Shulman, well-known architectural photographer, has said, "There are great individual moments everywhere that you move in the space of this cathedral." Quoted by David Gebhard and Robert Winter, *An Architectural Guidebook to Los Angeles*.

contemporary soul of the cathedral. They portray 135 saints and blesseds from around the world. Behind the **Baptismal Font** is a set of five tapestries that tell the story of Jesus' baptism by St. John in the River Jordan. They were created at **Flanders Tapestries** near **Bruges, Belgium**, by a new technique of placing the images directly onto the weavings. The neutral tones in the tapestries were inspired by Italian frescoes. The cotton cloth used is similar to the cotton that Egyptians used in the mummification process, which has survived for thousands of years.

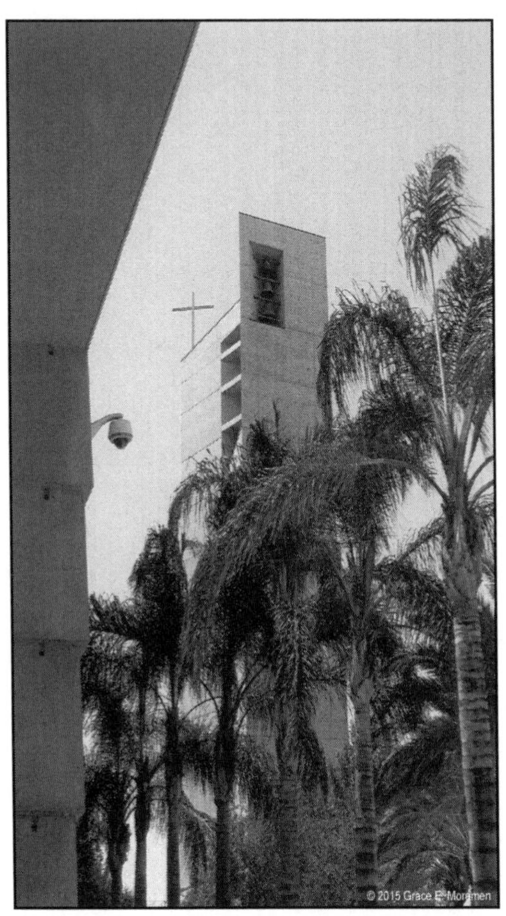

View of the Bell Tower at Our Lady of the Angels

The Dobson Pipe Organ Builders, Limited, of Lake City, Iowa, built the magnificent pipe organ. Vintage pipes from the organ in the **Cathedral of St. Vibiana** are included among the 6,019 pipes and 105 stops. This instrument is capable of playing different styles of music from the 1500s to the present. Listening to its tones, one can both *hear* the music and *feel* the vibrations in one's body and in the cathedral.

To return to Union Station from the Cathedral, **cross to the southeast corner of Temple and Grand Streets, and catch the Dash bus "B." Or, walk south on Hill Street one block to the Civic Center Metro Station; catch a train back to Union Station.**

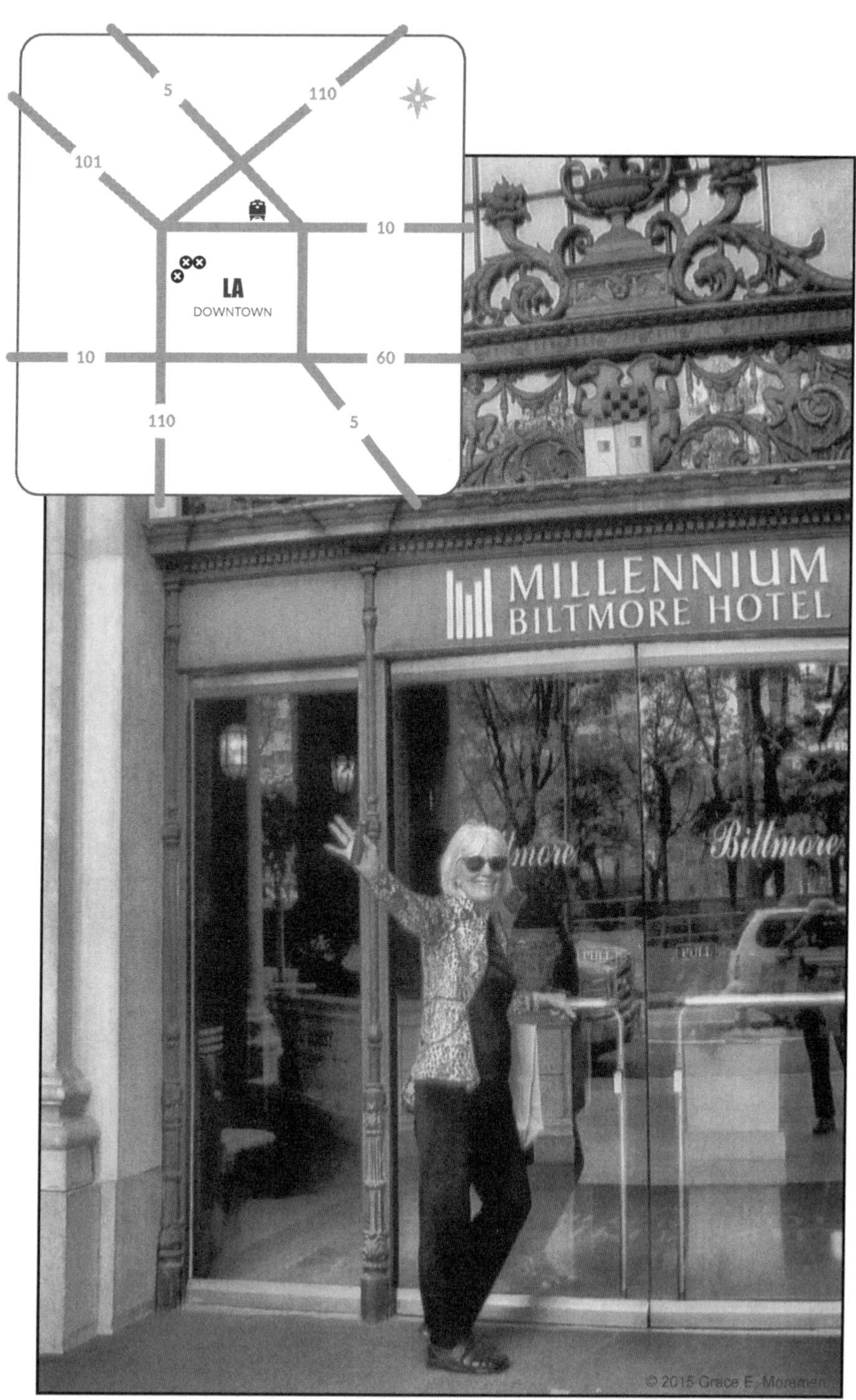
5
110
101
10
LA
DOWNTOWN
10
60
110
5
MILLENNIUM
BILTMORE HOTEL
Biltmore
© 2015 Grace E. Moreman

4

Knowledge and Elegance

LA Central Library • Fine Arts Building Millennium-Biltmore Hotel

*The **Pershing Square** area of downtown Los Angeles is home to all three of these historic landmarks. All were built in the 1920s, and are located within a few blocks of each other. A large and surprising mural is also located here.**

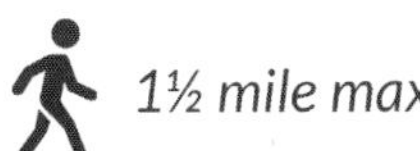 *1½ mile max*

 *3-4 hours*

 *no fees*

At Union Station catch the Metro Red or Purple Line and get off at Pershing Square. Take the Fifth Street exit and walk one block west to Fifth and Olive Streets. Look to your right (north) to see the world's largest abstract mural, ***Dusk***, by American artist **Frank Stella.**[1]

Continue on Fifth, past the Biltmore Hotel on your left (we will come back to that). Cross Grand Avenue. Notice the striking **Bunker Hill Steps** on the north side of the street. Make a left on Flower Street and you will come to the front of the library building and the magnificent **Maguire Gardens**. This most inviting public space has beautiful landscaping with several dramatic fountains and many sculptures. As you walk up the steps toward the entrance, notice the words in many languages written on the back of the steps.

1) The mural is part of Frank Stella's *"Moby Dick"* series and conceptually focuses on motion and travel. It occupies 40,000 square feet of the south and east walls of the Pacific Bell/AT&T building.

* Unless otherwise indicated, background information for Adventure 4 was provided by the LA Conservancy Walking Tours and the Central Library tour.

On your right in the far corner of the garden is the not to-be-missed **World Peace Bell**, dedicated in 2001 to the people and city of Los Angeles. It is comprised of coins and materials given by 103 countries as a symbol of world peace.[2]

The eight-story atrium in the Tom Bradley Wing

Architect **Bertram Grosvenor Goodhue** (1869–1924) designed the library building to incorporate several styles: *Byzantine, Egyptian, Modern, and Spanish.* It is crowned with a tower and a colorful, tiled pyramid. Goodhue's aim was to make people of all ages feel welcome and comfortable here. Although he did not live to see the library open in 1926, he succeeded in his goal. Today, 89 years later, one sees

2) www.publicartinla.com/LAPL/world_peace_bell.html

4

LA Central Library

630 West Fifth Street

213-228-7000 • www.lapl.org

Monday–Thursday: 10:00am–8:00pm

Friday–Saturday: 10:00am–5:30pm • Sunday: 1:00pm–5:30pm

© 2015 Grace E. Moremen

persons young and old and from every background making use of this wonderful facility. And it is delightful to see a child skipping along with mother or father, excited to be going to the library.

The second floor opens into a spacious rotunda. California's history is illustrated on the walls by a twelve-part mural by American artist **Dean Cornwell** (1892–1960), while the world is represented by a globe overhead that is contained within the chandelier.

Library tours are given every day of the week.

(No reservation is needed for groups of six or less.)

Building, Art, & Architecture Tour:

Monday–Saturday: 11:00am & 2:00pm • Sunday:2:00pm

***Garden Tour:** Saturday 12:30pm (times may change, check website)*

Just off the rotunda is the **Children's Literature Department**. This cheerful suite of rooms is well used by young people. Notice that the information desk is at a child's level. Each month there are many varied activities at the library for children, teens, and adults—for example, puppet shows on Saturdays. Check the website for current offerings.

Now walk to the east end of the corridor to the **Bradley Wing**. You may be amazed by the enormous, light-filled atrium that opens out before you. This eight-story addition was designed by **Norman Pfeiffer**, and named for the former, long-time mayor of Los Angeles, **Tom Bradley** (1917–1993). It was constructed after two arson fires in 1986 destroyed a third of the library's books. Notice the glass roof, the glass-walled reading rooms, and the escalators descending eight floors. Hanging from the ceiling are three fanciful chandeliers, designed by **Therman Satom**. It is said that the librarians call this wing, "the Grand Canyon of books."

The $260 million cost for this addition was creatively funded by the library's selling its air space to a developer who built the highest office building in Los Angeles across the street (the **US Bank Building**).

If you wonder whatever happened to the old card catalogues, be sure to ride the elevator, as the old cards line the elevator walls. One card catalogue is still in use in the Genealogy section of the library.

Exit the Library by way of the Fifth Street door which is just beyond the main checkout counter on the ground floor. Turn right on Fifth Street and walk down the hill to Olive Street. Turn right and walk to the entrance of the **Millennium-Biltmore Hotel**. You are looking at the city's oldest surviving luxury hotel, which opened in 1923.

Before you enter, take a moment to look up and observe the two sculptures, the Roman goddess Ceres on the right and the god Neptune on the left. Look down at the pavement and notice a compass set in brass. Its points–N, S, E, and W—are set at 45-degree angles, as stipulated by the ordinances of New Spain, which were in effect when the streets of Los Angeles were laid out in 1781 by **Philip de Neve**, the governor of the Californias at that time. (See Adventure 1)

Now for the ghost story. If you look up at the second floor you will notice the large windows. This was one of the grandest floors for guests when the hotel was built. When World War II came, the hotel generously turned these rooms over to servicemen to stay without charge

A welcoming place to relax and enjoy a beverage

Millennium-Biltmore Hotel

506 South Grand Avenue

213-624-1011

www.millenniumhotels.com/usa/millenniumbiltmorelosangeles

before they were shipped overseas. But when the war ended and the rooms were reopened to regular, paying customers, reports began coming back from guests about ghostly disturbances on that floor, so much so, that the entire floor was closed off, and remains so to this day.[3]

When you go into the hotel you are in the **Rendezvous Court**, the former main lobby until 1986, where high tea is served on weekends. But on any day it is a pleasant place to sit and enjoy a pot of tea, a glass of wine, or other beverages. This spacious room has a *Moorish*-style ceiling, Italian travertine stone walls and a wrought-iron stairway (a replica of one in the Cathedral in Burgos, Spain) that leads to the main areas of the hotel and its present lobby.

After mounting the stairs, you come into a long gallery, called the

3) LA Conservancy Walking Tour of the Biltmore Hotel.

Gallería Réal, the "King's Gallery," and its palatial scope is truly fit for a king. The ceiling frescoes were painted by renowned Italian muralist, **Giovanni Smeraldi**. Don't miss the "**Biltmore Angels**" that line the gallery. In fact, it is reported that there are angel motifs in every room of the hotel. The main lobby, once the Music Room, has a colossal skylight overhead that is definitely not to be missed. It has an *Art Deco* look befitting its 1923 date, and don't overlook the stunning *Art Deco* murals, by Southern California artist **Millard Sheets (1907–1989)**, that adorn each end of a seating alcove off the lobby.

Architects **Schulze and Weaver** designed their gleaming *Beaux Arts* palace to appeal to the rich and famous, and right from the beginning it attracted the leading lights of Hollywood. At its opening dinner in 1923, there were over 3,000 guests, including the leading movie producer, **Cecil B. DeMille** (1881–1959). Legend has it that the concept of an Academy of Motion Picture Arts and Sciences was born during a banquet in the hotel's Crystal Ballroom, and that the Oscar statuette was first sketched on a Biltmore Hotel napkin. Appropriately, the inaugural Academy Awards Ceremony in 1927 was held in that ballroom, and an old "Hollywood feel" still lingers in the hotel. Over the years, the Biltmore has been the set location for numerous films, such as *Chinatown*, *A Star is Born*, *Ocean's Eleven*, and *The Italian Job,* and on any given day, some of the rooms might be closed off due to filming. The Biltmore's architects were given carte blanche to design a luxury hotel. The result was spectacular in 1923, and it still endures as one of the sparkling gems of Los Angeles.

Exit the hotel through Rendezvous Court onto Olive Street and turn right. Walk to Seventh Street and make a right to 811 West Seventh Street to see the lobby of the *Romanesque*-style **Fine Arts Building** designed by **Albert Raymond Walker** and **Percy Augustus Walker**. Before you enter the building, look up and see the large reclining statues representing *sculpture* on the left, and *architecture* on the right. When you open the bronze door you will be in a low-lit

Fine Arts Building

811 West Seventh

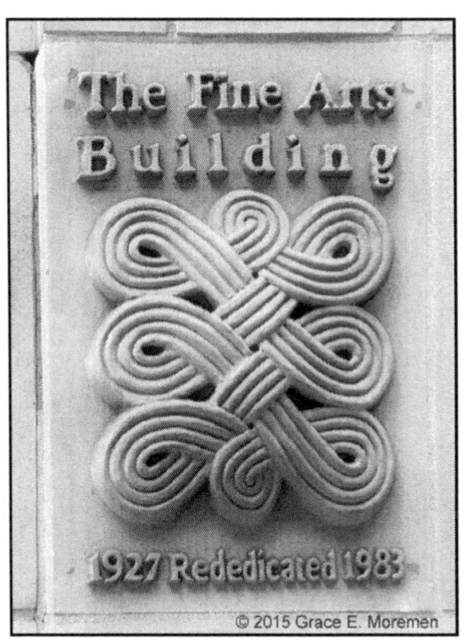

© 2015 Grace E. Moremen

two-story lobby, not unlike the nave of a grand cathedral. Chandeliers overhead send streams of light down to illuminate the room, and display cases line the walls, looking as though they should hold the relics of saints. Metal stars decorate the elevator doors, while ornate tiles cover the walls.[4]

Dominating the lobby is a shallow pool with bronze sculptures of children playing in the water. The little girl catching a slippery fish is modeled after the daughter of the sculptor, **Burt William Johnson** (1890–1927). He also sculpted the figures on the outside of the building.

The Fine Arts Building opened in 1926 with a reception and gala attended by several thousand guests who ignored a thunderstorm to attend. The event honored the architects of the building, which was dedicated to artists and artisans. Even though the Fine Arts Building has housed many different enterprises over the years, the stunning beauty of its lobby has survived.[5]

Walk back on Seventh Street to the **Seventh Street/Metro Center station.** Take the **Red or Purple Metro Line** to **Union Station.**

---

4) Ernest A. Batchelder (1875–1957), one of the leaders of the Arts and Crafts Movement, designed the tiles.
5) http://www.kcet.org/socal/departures/columns/lost-landmarks/the-fine-arts-building-art-artifice-and-illegal-operations.html

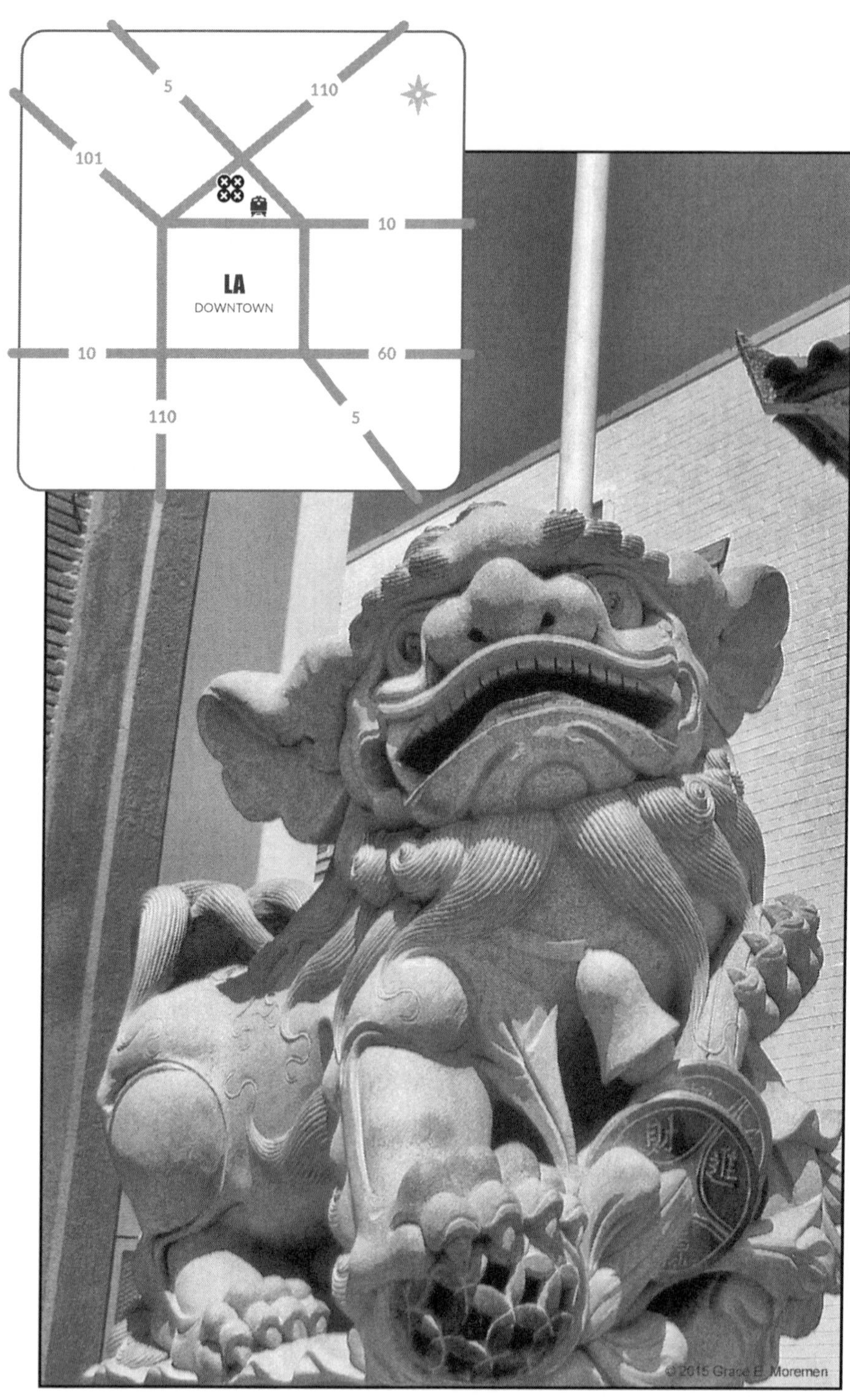
5
110
101
10
LA
DOWNTOWN
10
60
110
5
© 2015 Grace E. Moremen

5

A Resilient Neighborhood: Walking through Chinatown

Thien Hau Temple • West Plaza Central Plaza • Dragon Gate

***LA's Chinatown** is a fascinating and rewarding place to visit. **Located half a mile northwest of Union Station**, the area covers roughly twenty city blocks, and the resident population numbers about sixteen thousand. While it does have tourist attractions, Chinatown is also a busy neighborhood with residences, businesses, schools, temples, churches, a recreation center, library, and a medical center.*

2 miles max

2–3 hours

no fees

As was noted in Adventure 1, Los Angeles' Chinese community grew up over decades in the area near the railroad, east of Los Angeles Street. But in the 1930s, the community was forced to relocate elsewhere and many moved to land northwest of the original site. It is greatly to their credit that the resilient people of this community rallied and built a "second Chinatown."[1]

From **Union Station** take the **Gold Line north (direction Sierra Madre) and exit at the first stop**. Take time to appreciate the artful touches of Chinese décor in the station.

1) Succeeding generations have moved farther east to the Monterey Park area, creating a more contemporary "third Chinatown."

After you exit the station onto College Street, notice the massive, bronze ***Yong Bell,*** hanging in its own frame, across the street. It is a replica of a bell, 2,000 years old, that was unearthed in Guangzhou, China in 1983. Symbolizing peace and harmony, the beautiful blue-green bronze bell was a gift from Guangzhou to Los Angeles on the occasion of the 20th anniversary of their sister-city agreement.[2] Don't miss the tiny figure of a monkey perched on top of the bell who gazes cheerfully down at you!

Chua Ba Thien Hau Temple

750–756 North Yale

213-680-1860

Stay on College Street and walk west, up the hill, **for three blocks to Yale Street.** Turn left and proceed to the ***Chua Ba Thien Hau*** **Temple, 750–756 North Yale.** This handsome structure was erected in 2005 by the Chinese Vietnamese community. This is a Taoist temple that honors ***Thien Hau***, Goddess of the Sea, a deity especially dear to the Vietnamese "boat people" who escaped during the Vietnam War. In front of the temple stand several magnificent stone sculptures of horses and *fu* dogs, while dragons adorn the granite pillars of the porch. Upon

2) *Angel Walk*. Los Angeles Department of Cultural Affairs, 2005.

entering the temple, your senses are immediately engaged by the sight of brilliant red and gold decoration, the scent of incense lit to offer prayers, and the insistent sound of a gong being gently struck at regular intervals; all seem to invite you to stop and contemplate the divine.[3]

Exit the temple and walk right (north) on Yale to **Castelar Elementary School.** On one of its outside walls you will see a lively and sprightly **mural of children playing "Ring Around the Rosy,"** painted in 1977 by **Leo Politi.**[4] It might surprise you to know that this school, dating from 1882, is the second oldest public school in the city. Located in a formerly Italian neighborhood, one of Castelar's most famous graduates was movie director Frank Capra (*It's a Wonderful Life).* Today, the multicultural enrollment is about 1,000, and the school provides faculty and staff who speak all major languages and Asian dialects.

West Plaza

Chun King Road

Moving on, **proceed to Chung King Road and turn right.** This narrow road connects to **West Plaza,** an area of artists' studios and galleries. **Fong's Oriental Works of Art** is located here, established by Fong See in 1952, and still owned by the family. On the Plaza, look for the tranquil white marble statue of ***Guanyin***, the Buddhist Goddess of Mercy and Compassion, located under an arbor.

Ahead, directly across Hill Street, you will see the **West Gate** that gives access to the **Central Plaza, the prime tourist center of Chinatown.** Parts of the gate are constructed of camphor wood

3) Other places of worship in Chinatown include a Confucian temple, the Chinese United Methodist Church, the Chinese First Baptist Church, and two Catholic churches.

4) Leo Politi was a well-known children's book author and illustrator who wrote about Los Angeles. Another of his murals, *The Blessing of the Animals,* adorns a building on the Old Plaza. (Adventure 1)

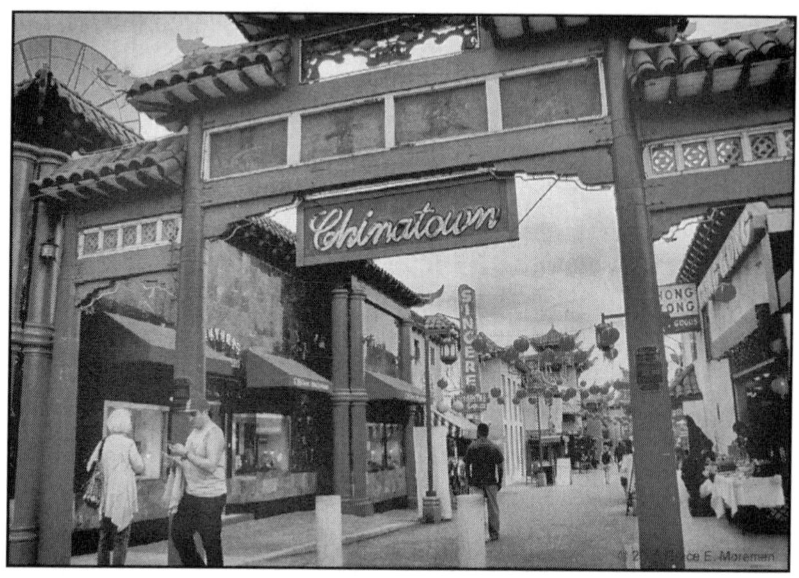

West Gate • Central Plaza

Hill Street

imported from China, said to be 150 years old. It is the neighborhood's earliest gate, built in 1938 for New Chinatown's grand opening. An inscription at the top of the gate reads "Cooperate to Achieve" in Chinese characters. During the opening ceremonies, the **Governor of California, Frank Merriam**, dedicated a bronze plaque at this site commemorating the contributions of the Chinese people to the building of the railroads.

After going through the gate, and passing shops and restaurants, you will come to the **Central Plaza**, the locale for festivities such as Chinese New Year and summer evening concerts. Movies and TV episodes are often filmed here. Just ahead you will see the impressive statue of **Dr. Sun Yat Sen** (1866–1925), the first president of the Republic of China;[5] it faces the East Gate, so it may be seen immediately by those who enter from that direction.

5) Dr. Sun, a Chinese revolutionary, visited Los Angeles in 1905 to gather support for an uprising against the corrupt Qing Dynasty. Some scholars believe that he might not have been successful in overthrowing the Manchus had it not been for this early support from the Chinese community in Los Angeles.

Now look to your left and notice the colorful mural of a mystical looking dragon by renowned Chinese American artist **Tyrus Wong.**[6] Did you know that Mr. Wong is also the artist who painted the lovely woodland scenes for Walt Disney's movie, *Bambi?* It is fitting that the image of the dragon is near the gate, because in Chinese folk tradition, dragons represent guardians endowed with strength and goodness, power and benevolence.

You may notice that many of the rooftops in the Central Plaza are outlined with neon lights. They will be lighted on weekends and special occasions. If you can arrange it, it is worth staying after dark to experience the brilliant green, red, and gold lights—a magnificent sight to see![7]

East Gate Plaza

Broadway

Exit through the splendid East Gate. It is one of the most recognizable landmarks in Los Angeles. Called the **Gate of Maternal Virtues,** it is dedicated to the memory of all mothers.

You are now on North Broadway, Chinatown's main business concourse. Turning right (south) you will see the imposing exterior of the **Chinese Consolidated Benevolent Association,** guarded by two fierce *fu* dogs. Benevolent associations mediate between individuals and organizations, fight against discriminatory laws, and serve as a political voice for the Chinese-American community.

A short way farther south, high on the façade of the building at **911 North Broadway, look for three enormous tile murals** that resemble traditional Chinese scrolls. They are believed to be the largest tile murals outside of China.

There are several Chinese herbal dispensaries on Broadway, and you

6) Tyrus Wong immigrated from China as a boy. He exhibited great artistic ability and graduated from the Otis Art Institute in Los Angeles. Later he became a prominent artist with Disney Studios. In recent years, Mr.Wong has built and flown a great number of extraordinary kites. At this writing, he is still active at 104 years of age. Grace has had the pleasure of meeting him.

7) Chinatown at night is one of the venues on the Neon Cruise. (Adventure 13)

East Gate

will see shops established by the Vietnamese and other Asian immigrants. As a final stop, you might want to try the **Far East Plaza at 727 North Broadway**, a two-story mall that offers a great variety of merchandise, including a specialized tea emporium. Try sampling some of the teas offered. The variety is astounding.

If you are there in mid-day, you might like to have lunch at a *dim sum* restaurant. Two examples are **Ocean Seafood Restaurant** and the **Empress Pavillion**, both on Hill Street. However, there are many other choices of places to eat.

For your return to Union Station, turn off Broadway onto College Street and walk back to the Gold Line Station. Catch a southbound train marked "East LA" and go one stop.

Or, you can keep walking south on Broadway. Up ahead is the magnificent **Dragon Gate**, Chinatown's newest portal. It was designed by **Rupert Mok** and installed in 2001. You can see LA City Hall in the distance, giving a feeling of connectedness between Chinatown and

the Civic Center. **At the intersection of Broadway and Cesar Chavez Avenue,** you will walk under the dragons, four stories above you! The male and female dragons are competing for the moon, represented by a white globe that stands between them. In addition to their other attributes, dragons also symbolize good luck, prosperity, and longevity. This pair seems to beckon visitors to Chinatown, even as they stand guard over the Chinese-American community of Los Angeles.

Palace in Heaven (anonymous, 1968, 913 N. Broadway)

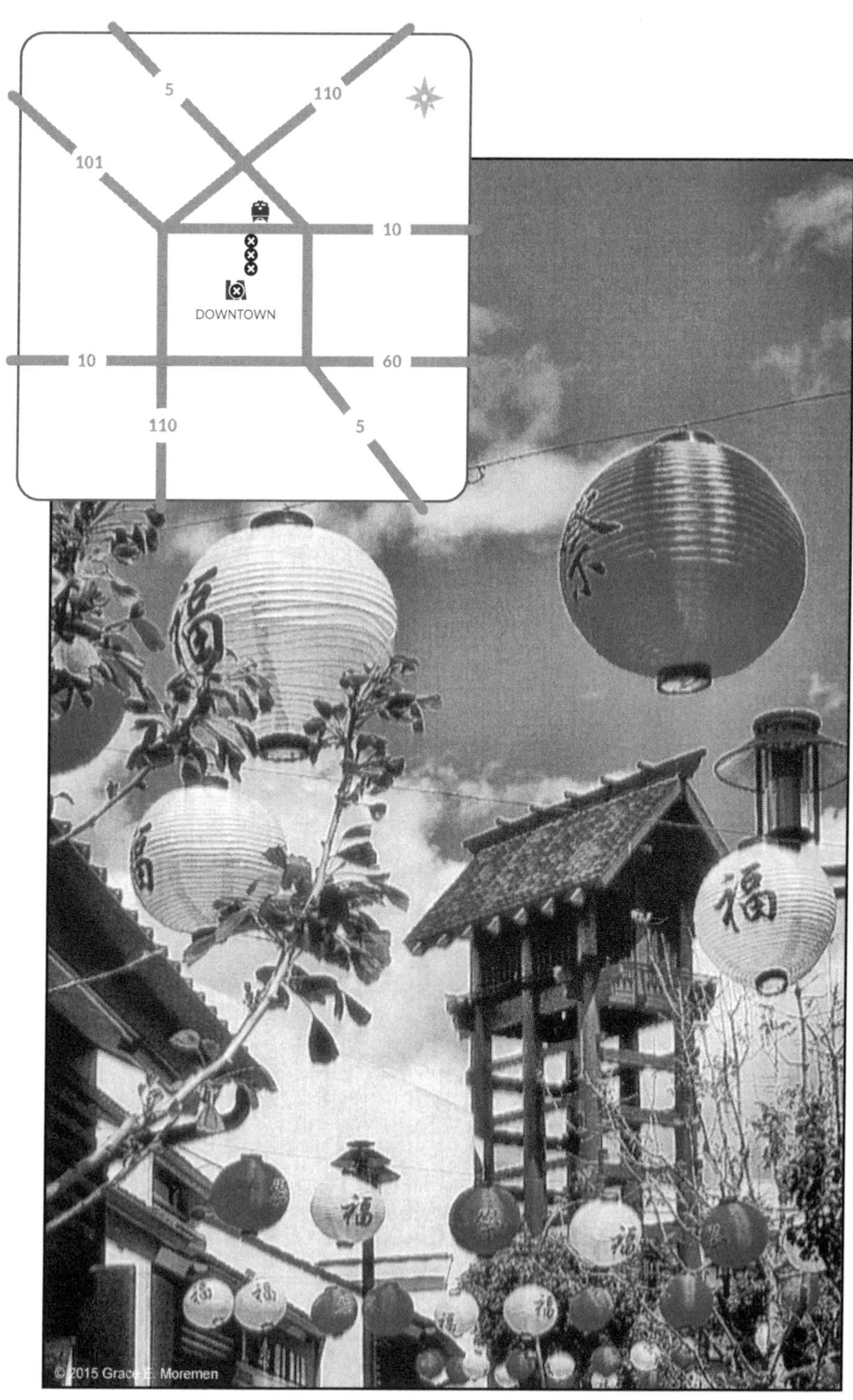
5
110
101
10
DOWNTOWN
10
60
110
5
福
© 2015 Grace E. Moremen

Blossoms and a History Lesson

LA Flower District • Little Tokyo Japanese American National Museum Geffen Contemporary Art Museum

*This Adventure is full of the color and fragrances of the **Flower Market** and the liveliness and rich cultural history of Little Tokyo.**

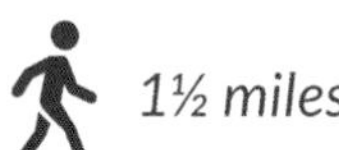

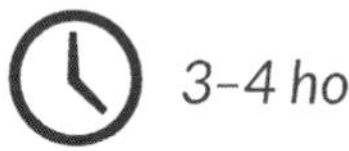

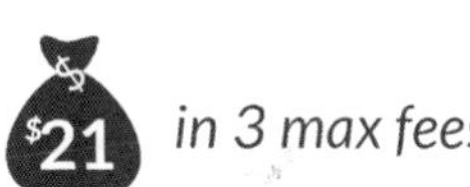

From Union Station, **take the Metro (either the Red or Purple line) to Seventh Street/Metro Center. Walk east on Seventh Street one block to Hope Street. Look for the stop for the Dash Bus "E."** Show your Metrolink ticket for a **free ride to Los Angeles Street where you exit the bus.** The specific Flower Market buildings we will visit are located off Seventh Street between Maple and Wall Street.[1]

To get there, **walk two blocks east on Seventh and make a right on Maple Street. The entrance to our chosen Flower Market is halfway down the block on your left.**

1) The wholesale flower district covers many blocks, with over one hundred vendors. We chose this route because of its relative accessibility for pedestrians using public transportation.
* Unless otherwise indicated, background information for Adventure 6 is from the Japanese American National Museum and *Downtown Los Angeles: A Walking Guide* by Robert D. Herman, 2004.

Southern California Flower Market

754 & 755 Wall Street

laflowerdistrict.com

Public Hours - Monday: 8:00am–12:00noon • Tuesday: 6:00am–11:00am
Wednesday: 8:00am–12:00noon • Thursday: 6:00am–12:00noon
Friday: 8:00am–2:00pm • Saturday: 6:00am–2:00pm • Closed Sunday
Cost: $2 Monday–Friday • $1 on Saturday

Plan to arrive around 10:00am, as there are fewer shoppers at that time. The wholesaler tradespeople shop between 2:00am and 8:00am. The enormous expanse of floor space and variety of flowers can be quite overwhelming as you shop from one building to the other. Your purchases will be well wrapped and protected to survive a long day. The wholesale flower district experience is unique and delightful.

From the Flower Market, **return to Seventh Street, turn left, and proceed to Main Street.** You are looking for the stop for **Dash Bus "D," which is on the southeast corner. Buses run every five minutes during the day until 6:00pm. Disembark at Third Street and walk one block north to Vibiana at 214 S. Main Street.** The former St. Vibiana's Cathedral of Los Angeles was designed by **Ezra F. Keysor** in the *Italianate* style.[2] It opened in 1876, making it the oldest surviving building in this part of the city.[3] Today it is used as an event space

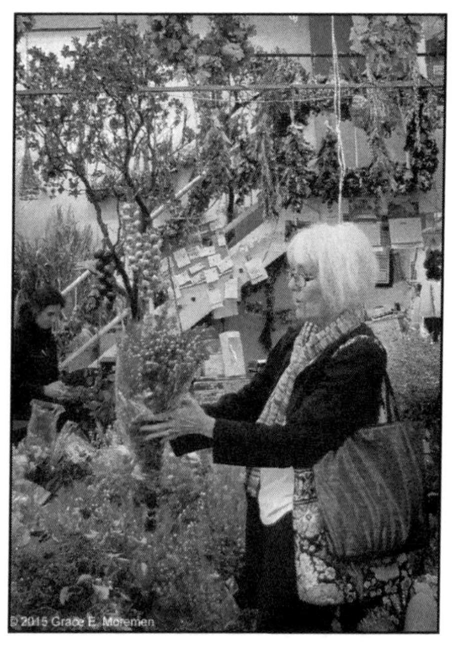
©2015 Grace E. Moremen

2) Keysor also designed the Pico House on the Old Plaza. (Adventure 1)

3) St. Vibiana's was severely damaged in the Northridge earthquake on January 17, 1994. A new cathedral, Our Lady of the Angels, was built farther west and opened in 2002. (Adventure 3)

owned by the City of Los Angeles. To inquire about visiting the building and garden, go to Vibiana.com or call 213-626-1517.

After passing Vibiana, walk to the corner of Second and Main streets and turn right on Second. You are now entering **Little Tokyo,** an attractive and friendly neighborhood enriched by public art, shops, restaurants, and two major museums. Little Tokyo is the cultural center for the largest Japanese American community in North America, and was declared a national Historic Landmark in 1995. Not a large area, it is situated (approximately) between First Street on the north, Third Street on the south, Main Street on the west, and the LA River on the east.

Walk east on Second Street. You will come to the entrance of a pedestrian thoroughfare named Onizuka Street that runs diagonally

Walking into Japanese Village Plaza, the heart of Little Tokyo, from Second Street

between Second and First Street. Note the startling white fiberglass sculpture, *Friendship Knot,* at the entrance to the street.[4] Turn left onto Onizuka Street; ahead you can't miss the large, impressive monument to Japanese American astronaut **Ellison S. Onizuka** (1946–1986), a mission specialist aboard the Space Shuttle *Challenger* that disintegrated upon takeoff on January 28, 1986. A scale model of the *Challenger* is part of the memorial.

At this point, you can either retrace your steps back to Second Street, or turn left on First and continue to the **Double Tree Hotel** on the corner of First and Los Angeles streets. There you will find a delightful place for a relaxing break: **the roof garden on the south wing of the Double Tree Hotel at 120 South Los Angeles Street.** Stroll through waterfalls and the quiet and serene garden landscape, while viewing the lively city below.

4) *Friendship Knot,* measuring 18′ 4″ in height, was created by Shinkichi Tajiri in 1972 and was dedicated in 1981 as a memorial to Dr. Morinorsuke Kajima. (www.publicartinla.com/Downtown/Little_Tokyo/friendship_knot.html)

Return to Onizuka Street, turn right, and walk to the conjunction of Onizuka and San Pedro streets. Walk south on San Pedro to the **Japanese American Cultural and Community Center, on your left at 224 San Pedro Street. Isamu Noguchi** designed the brick-paved plaza, and in the center is one of his installations. ***To the Issei*** has two massive hewn boulders on a raised brick platform, one standing upright, symbolizing the heroic energy of humankind, and one lying horizontally, symbolizing repose. In the plaza there is also the 880-seat **Japan American Theatre** that offers Kabuki dances and contemporary plays about the Japanese American experience.

Across from the theatre is the **James Irvine Memorial Garden** with its ***Garden of the Clear Stream.*** Descend the steps and stroll through this beautiful and peaceful garden with its flowing stream, redwoods and Japanese black pines, wooden bridges, and elegant stone lanterns. **Hours:** Tuesday–Friday from 10:00am–5:00pm. (Note that the garden hours are subject to change without notice.)

Return to the brick-paved plaza and enter the **Japanese American Cultural and Community Center.** Here art exhibits are often displayed, and the day we were there we enjoyed seeing an exhibit of the ancient **Japanese art of Shikishi.** This form of art blends painting with poetry, sometimes referred to as "poem cards," which can range from the elegant to the whimsical.

Go back to San Pedro Street and walk north to Second. Just north of Second is the attractive **Japanese Village Plaza,** a mini outdoor mall featuring shops and restaurants that runs between Second and First streets. Notice the metal plates covering the ground around the trees that feature raised, sculptured gingko leaves embedded in the metal. The effect is stunning. Up ahead on First Street you can see the Little Tokyo **Watch Tower** (also visible from the Observation Deck at **LA City Hall,** Adventure 3). The tower may look wooden and fragile but it is actually a sturdy metal structure.

Children gather around *The Cube* in front of the museum.

Walk to your right (east) on First Street. A number of buildings from the turn of the twentieth century have survived along this block, including a building in the *Beaux Arts* style erected in 1896 (now home of the Far East Café). **The Japanese American National History Museum is straight ahead of you.**

In the plaza in front of the museum you will see the **OOMO: LA Cube (*Out Of Many One*).** The Cube, by artist **Nicole Maloney,** is an interactive art installation and part of a citywide campaign to change the world one picture at a time. The different moveable parts of the cube make it especially appealing to young people on school trips. One side of the cube is made of aluminum and reflects whatever is in front of it. By turning the cube around, different configurations can be made and you can see yourself in the reflection. Take a selfie!

The **Japanese American National Museum,** established in 1992, is dedicated to preserving the history of Japanese Americans. Its permanent exhibit, ***Common Ground: The Heart of Community,*** includes the early days of the Issei (first-generation) pioneers through World War II,

6

Japanese American National Museum

100 North Central Avenue
213-625-0414 • janm.org

Tuesday • Wednesday • Friday–Sunday: 11:00am–5:00pm
Thursday: 12:00noon–8:00pm • Closed Monday
Adults: $9 • Seniors (62+): $5
Students (with ID) & Youth (6–17): $5
Free all-day general admission every **third** Thursday of the month
Free every Thursday evening from 5:00pm to 8:00pm

the incarceration period, and up to the present. Haunting is the wall of suitcases from the internment camp experience, and the many other objects and photographs on display that remind us of that dark time in our nation's history. The incarceration and internment of Japanese during World War II greatly affected Little Tokyo. Prior to that, the district had been home to some 35,000 Japanese Americans. After the war many did not return to this district to live. However, a large number of Japanese reestablished their businesses and cultural enterprises here. The result has been an impressive rebirth of Little Tokyo.

This museum also has excellent special exhibitions that are beautifully displayed. Recent examples are ***Dodgers: Brotherhood of the Game,*** featuring several Japanese players, and an exhibit devoted to the Japanese marketing phenomenon ***Hello Kitty.*** Another show featured the ***Art of Japanese Tattooing,*** a surprisingly beautiful art form, going back centuries.

After leaving the Japanese American National Museum, turn right (north) and the **Geffen Contemporary at MOCA** is next door.[5]

5) David Lawrence Geffen, a billionaire philanthropist, was a major benefactor of this museum.

Geffen Museum of Contemporary Art

152 N. Central Avenue

213-626-6222 • moca.org

Monday: 11:00am–5:00pm

Thursday: 11:00am–8:00pm

Friday: 11:00am–5:00pm

Saturday and Sunday: 11:00am–6:00pm

Free Thursday evenings: 5:00pm–8:00pm

Closed Tuesday and Wednesday, and major holidays

Adults $12 • Students with ID: $7 • Seniors (65+): $7

Children under 12: Free • Jurors with ID: Free

(Present a valid TAP card and receive a two-for-one general admission.)

Free Exhibition Highlight Tours every Thursday:

5:00pm • 6:00pm • 7:00pm

Saturday and Sunday: 12:00noon • 1:00pm • 2:00pm • 3:00pm

Wheelchairs and strollers are available at the front desk on a first-come, first-served basis.

The Geffen Contemporary at MOCA is one of three locations that comprise the entire Museum of Contemporary Art (see Adventure 2). This site has an interesting history. A police-car warehouse in its former life, it boasts 40,000 square feet of floor space. It was redesigned as an art museum by local architect **Frank O. Gehry** (who also designed the Walt Disney Concert Hall). The Geffen at MOCA opened in 1979 and is often used to display particularly large pieces of art. MOCA's permanent collection, which is still growing, is considered to be one of the country's finest concentrations of American and European art created since 1940.

Onizuka Street, looking northwest toward City Hall

To return to Union Station—an easy ride on Metro—**walk east on First Street one block to Alameda.** You will see the **Gold Line Station** to your left. Catch a **northbound train marked "Sierra Madre"** and get off at **Union Station, the first stop.**

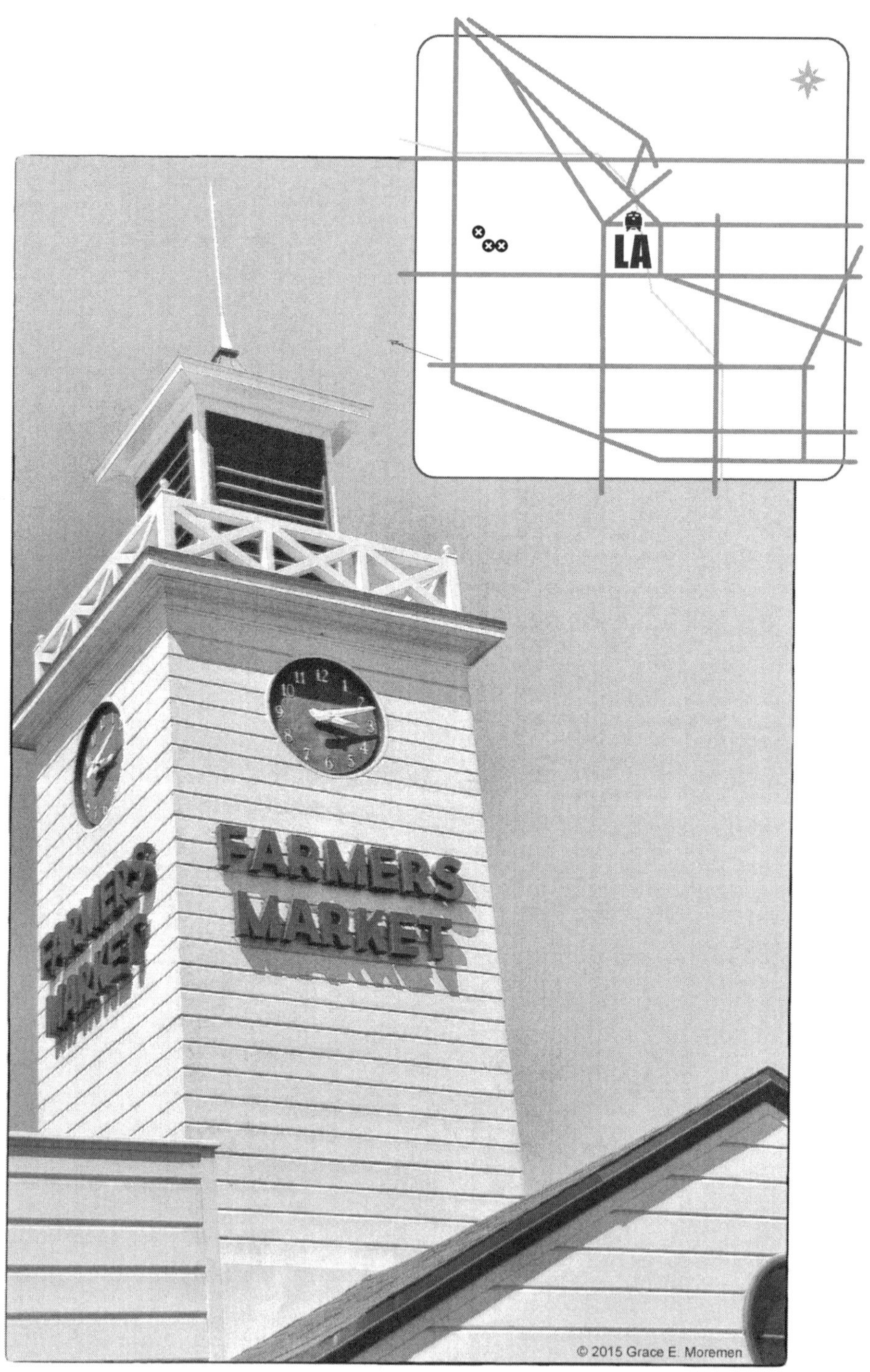
LA
FARMERS MARKET
© 2015 Grace E. Moremen

Mammoths and Munchies

Page Museum • La Brea Tar Pits
Farmers Market

Thirty thousand years ago, mammoths (gigantic elephant-like creatures with long curved tusks) roamed the marsh-lands of what would become the Los Angeles basin. Along with a few of their contemporaries, such as dire wolves and saber-toothed cats, some unfortunate mammoths met their end in pits of tar. Since early in the twentieth century, paleontologists have been excavating the fossilized remains of these ancient animals, and the work still goes on today. A true LA landmark, the La Brea Tar Pits have a fascinating story which is well told by a film and exhibits at the Page Museum, located on site. Then, for a complete change of pace, come back to the present day and visit the nearby Farmers Market—an LA "institution"—and a delightful place to eat and shop!

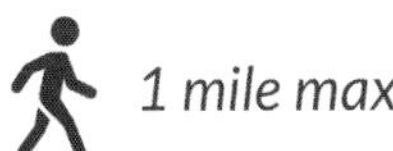

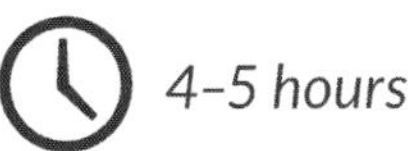

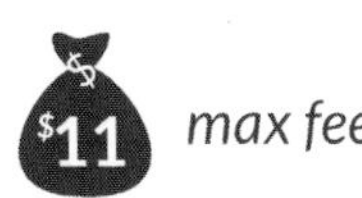

From Union Station take the Metro Red Line and get off at Vermont Avenue. Take any **#720 Rapid red bus (westbound)** on Wilshire. Get off at Fairfax and walk a short way back, past LACMA. to the Page Museum and Tar Pits.

In the museum, first **view a short film in the theater** for an overview of the exhibits and the history of the excavations.

Page Museum • La Brea Tar Pits

5801 Wilshire Boulevard

323-857-6300 • tarpits.org

General Admission: $11

Seniors and Youth 13–17: $8 • Children 5–12: $5

Open Daily 9:30am–5:00pm

Closed: New Year's Day, 4th of July, Thanksgiving, Christmas

Docents can show you the tooth of the Columbian mammoth, one similar to a modern day elephant's tooth. You can also view an exhibition about the dire wolf and the saber-toothed cat, and many birds including the golden eagle and the heron. One of the most surprising and amazing exhibitions is the "Fishbowl Laboratory," where one can look through a window and observe some of the museum's paleontologists at work on fossils.

There are several tar pits along the walkways on the grounds of the Page Museum. After visiting the museum, take a walking tour of these

The scene at the La Brea Tar Pits with the Page Museum in the backdrop.

7

pits and the **Pleistocene Garden** that features plants from the last Ice Age. Notice the bubbles in the dark, tarry water. They are formed by methane gas escaping from the depths. In one area, the older excavations of pits 3, 4, 61, and 67, ancient camels, bison, and horses were found. Pit 9 is considered the oldest site, where thirty individual mammoth fossils came to light in 1914. That was also the year when digging began in Pit 13, and many fossils from that site are on display in the museum. Pit 91 is a viewing station that is open daily from 10am to 4pm Project 23 is the area where excavators are currently working seven days a week.

Walk back to Fairfax Avenue and catch the #217 Local bus (northbound).

Mammoth skeleton and dioramas in the Page Museum.

Farmers Market

6333 West Third Street

323-933-9211 • farmersmarketla.com

Toll Free 866-993-9211

Hours: Mon–Fri • 9:00am–9:00pm;

Sat 9:00am–8:00pm • Sun 10:00am–7:00pm

(Note: Some merchants have extended hours)

Get off at Third Street and walk to a most lively, aromatic, bustling market—the original Farmers Market, established in 1934. In the early days, Angelenos could buy directly from local farmers who parked their trucks here. Today over 100 venues offer everything from hand-made ice cream and old-time chewing gum, to fresh produce, vintage memorabilia, and much more. Over thirty restaurants offer dishes from Mexico, Greece, Italy, France, and Asia. For American food,

Jacqueline ponders a melon at The Farmers Market.

go to **Dupar's, famous for their pies**. Dupar's bakery provides samples, allowing you to taste before making your choice to take home for supper—oh, so good! Grace's favorite sight at the Farmers Market is the peanut butter machine; it's fun to watch, and the result is delicious.

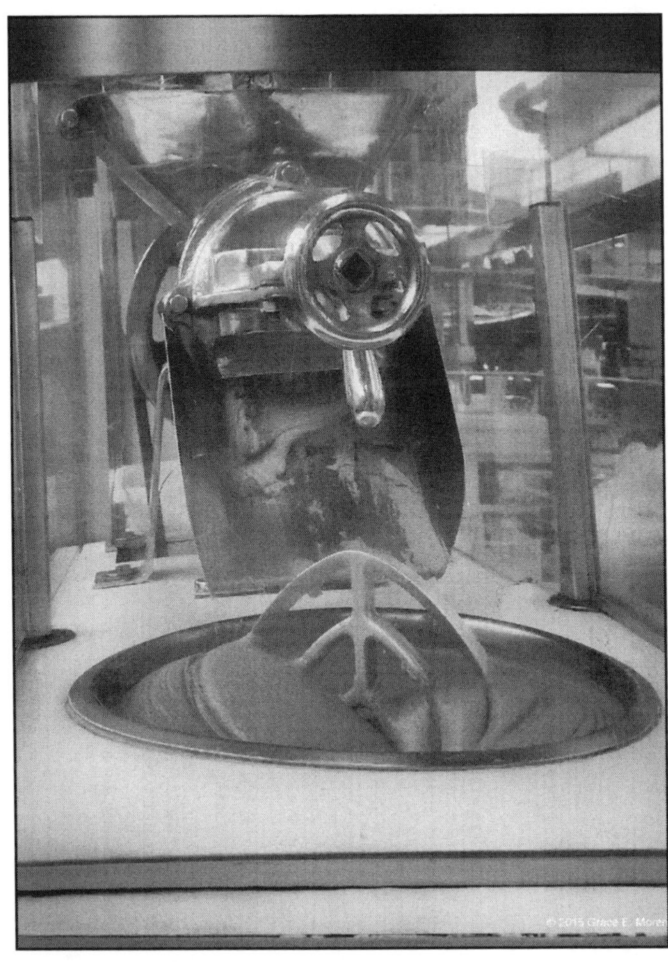

To return to Union Station, walk back to **Fairfax** and **cross to the west side.** Look for the bus stop for the **southbound #217 Local bus.** Get off at **Wilshire Boulevard.** Cross Wilshire and take the **#720 Rapid (red bus) eastbound.** Get off at **Western.** Take the **Metro back to Union Station.**

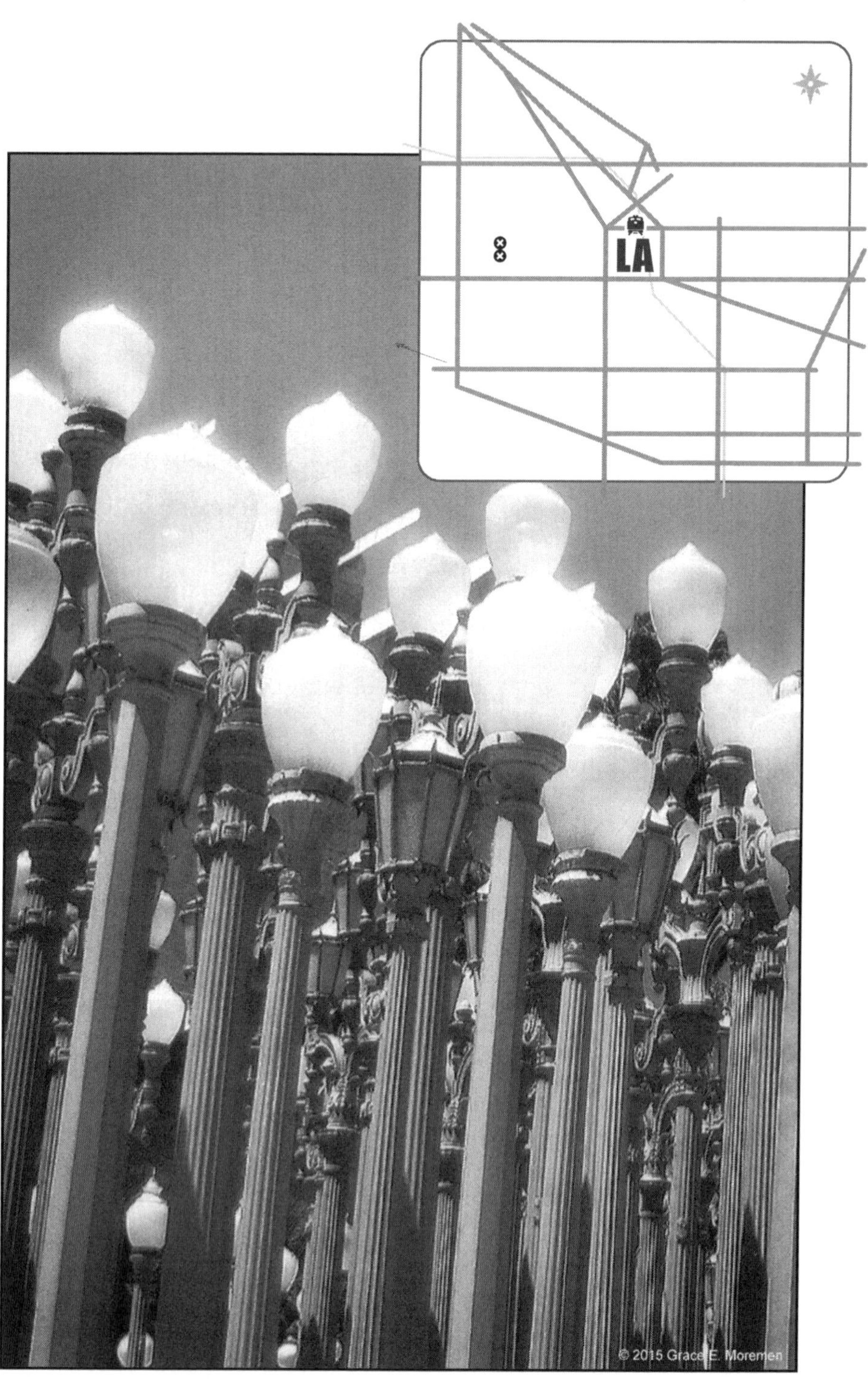
LA
© 2015 Grace E. Moremen

8

A Grand Cultural Embrace

LA County Museum of Art (LACMA)
The Petersen Automotive Museum

For a rich day of rewarding and inspiring encounters with the visual arts and the art of the automobile, a visit to the Los Angeles County Museum of Art and the Petersen Automotive Museum is a must. Located across Wilshire Boulevard from each other, these two different, but complementary, venues can easily be combined.

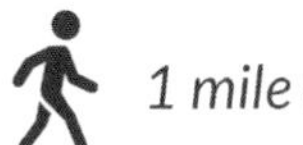

From Union Station, take the **Purple Line** and get off at the **Wilshire/Western Station.** Catch the **Rapid #720 Red** bus on Wilshire Boulevard. It is free with your Metrolink ticket or Day Pass. Travel west on Wilshire Boulevard for about five miles. Get off at the **Fairfax** stop and walk a short way back to **LACMA.**

Los Angeles's largest art museum (and the largest art museum in the western United States) began its life in 1913 with a few galleries at the Natural History Museum at Exposition Park. In 1961 it was established as a separate entity and opened at its present location on Wilshire Boulevard in Hancock Park in 1965. Its collection numbers over 120,000 objects that range from antiquity to the present day. Among its strengths are Asian art, Latin American art—from

LACMA

5905 Wilshire Boulevard (at Fairfax Avenue)
323-857-6000 • lacma.org
Monday, Tuesday, & Thursday: 11:00am–5:00pm •
Friday: 11:00am–8:00pm •
Saturday & Sunday: 10:00am–7:00pm • Closed Wednesday
$15 Adults • $10 Seniors (62+) and students (18+) with ID

Free every day for members and children under 18.
Also free on the second Tuesday of each month and for LA County residents after 3:00pm every open weekday.
Children under 17 and one adult receive free museum membership and family art-making activities through LACMA's NexGen program.

Closed: New Year's Day, 4th of July, Thanksgiving, Christmas

pre-Columbian masterpieces to works by leading modern and contemporary artists—and Islamic art, of which LACMA hosts one of the most significant collections in the world.

Its signature installation, ***Urban Light,*** by American artist **Chris Burden,** immediately attracts the attention of visitors arriving on Wilshire Boulevard. This "forest" of 202 restored, antique streetlamps are a favorite venue for people of all ages as they move freely among the lamps.

There are many outdoor art installations at LACMA, such as ***Auguste*** by **Auguste Rodin** (1840–1917), and don't miss the **mobiles** by **Alexander Calder** (1898–1976) located in a pond on the east side of the campus. In fact, art pieces are located everywhere on the grounds,

so keep your eyes peeled. Look for ***Band*** by multimedia American artist **Richard Serra** and, inside the Ahmanson Building, ***La Gerbe*** (The Sheaf) by **Henri Matisse** (1869–1954), a large ceramic that is akin to his colorful collages made from cutouts.

All outdoor areas at LACMA are easily accessible and free of charge. Some grand views of the surrounding area are possible, too. For instance, from the east deck outside the cafe, one can see LACMA's next-door neighbor, the **La Brea Tar Pits,** and from the observation deck on the third floor of the **Broad Contemporary Art Building,** one can spy the famous **Hollywood sign** on the distant hills to the north. In the elevator on your way up, enjoy a massive work of graphic art by American feminist artist **Barbara Kruger.**

The **Japanese Pavilion** offers visitors a meditative experience that can be very welcome in the midst of the bustling city. The opaque lighting in this building lends itself to a reflective and quieting mood. Walk up and down the circular ramp to take in the exhibitions on each floor. The smallest works of art at LACMA in the **Raymond and Frances Bushell Netsuke Gallery.** They are called ***netsuke***—wonderful little toggles created to anchor the cord that holds a small purse carried under the ***obi*** (sash) on a ***kimono.*** Originally, they were simple, round, and compact. But over the years in the eighteenth and nineteenth centuries, they developed into an exquisite miniature art form called ***katabori,*** many carved from ivory. This was the golden age of *netsuke* production when the most artistic, decorative creations were fashioned. Look for the ***Kissing Geese,*** the ***Grazing Horse,*** or the ***Snail on Boar Tusk.*** Find your favorite![1] The *netsuke* are housed in their own exhibition space, created especially for them, that is located directly behind the Information Desk on the ground floor. One hundred and fifty of these tiny wonders are always on display. Each thematic exhibition lasts for a few months.

Now, from the smallest art works, go out to see the museum's largest object: ***Levitated Mass*** by American artist **Michael Heizer,** situated at

1) http://collections.lacma.org/node/424298

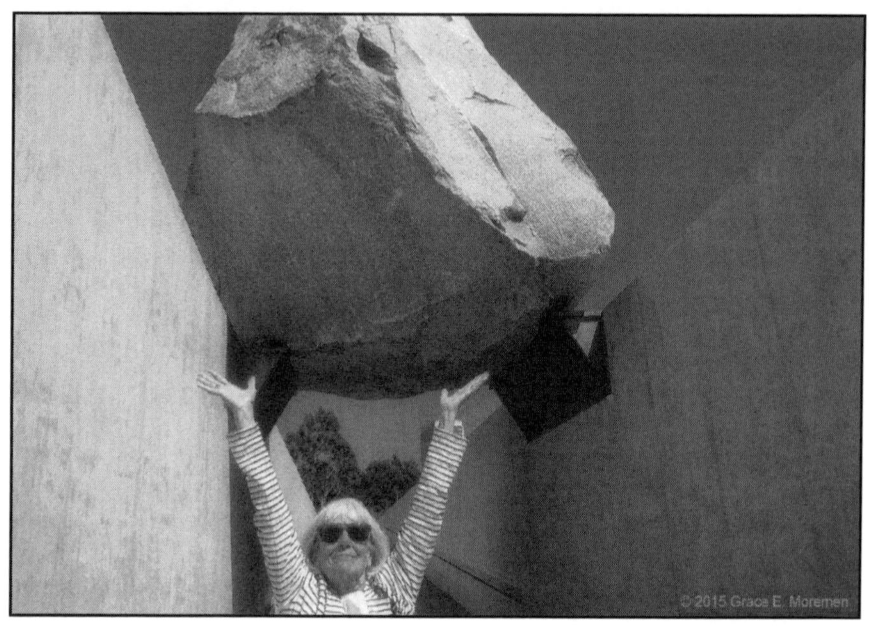

the northwest corner of the grounds near Third Street. Installed in 2012, this large-scale sculpture is, in fact, a 340-ton boulder, anchored over a concrete trench, allowing you to walk under it. Take a photo of a friend or yourself "holding it up"!

There are always special and outstanding exhibitions in place at LACMA, some of which require an extra entrance fee and advance reservations. Check the museum's website. In addition, there are daily Family Art activities in **Boone Children's Gallery** and occasional art classes. LACMA also presents films, concerts, and educational programs at various times during the year. Free LACMA tours are given daily at 1:00, 1:30, 2:00, and 3:00pm. To plan your visit, go to the website for further information. And don't forget to check out the three cafés at LACMA—all offer delicious meals or snacks.

The newly renovated **Petersen Automotive Museum** on the Miracle Mile at **Fairfax and Wilshire Boulevard** will present a dramatic sight when renovations are complete, with its long ribbons of stainless steel,

8

The Petersen Automotive Museum

660 Wilshire Boulevard

323-930-2277 • petersen.org

Reopens November 1, 2015

evoking the imagery of speed and the organic curves of an automobile. Light emanating from inside the building at night will accentuate the steel sculpture and act as a beacon. Most certainly, it will add dramatically to the architecture of Los Angeles. The Petersen's vast collection of automobiles and other motorized vehicles, many once owned by celebrities, is world class. Their colorful exhibits may be counted upon to entertain and educate visitors of all ages and interests.

For your return, catch the **#720 Rapid eastbound** bus on Wilshire. **Transfer at Western to the Metro and take the subway back to Union Station.**

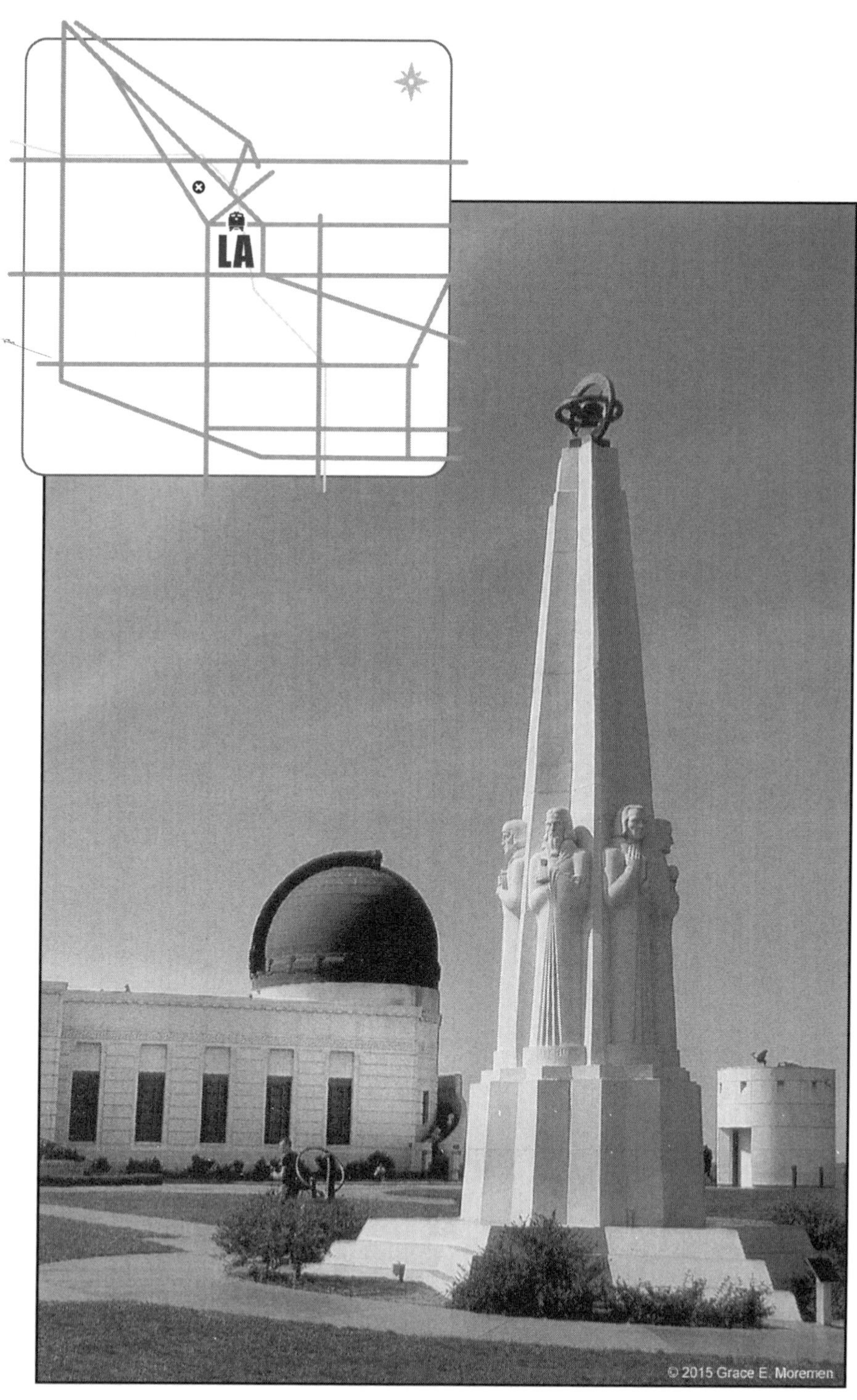
LA
© 2015 Grace E. Moremen

9

Hilltop Stargazer

The Griffith Observatory

On weekends, this hilltop destination is totally accessible by public transportation. (During the week, a car will be necessary. Limited parking is available.)

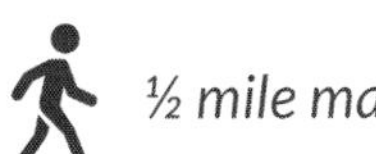
½ mile max

4 hours

max fee

The **Griffith Observatory** is one of the most beloved destinations in LA for all ages.[1] Perched 1,134 feet above sea level on the southern slope of Mount Hollywood, the domes of this beautiful *Art Deco*-style building are visible for miles around. Designed by **John C. Austin** and **F. M. Ashley,** it opened in 1935 and was renovated and expanded in 2002, and today it offers a state-of-the-art "immersive plantetarium environment." Its exciting and beautifully presented exhibits and theater shows reveal many secrets of our planet, outer space, and the universe. Free public telescopes on the observation deck are available every evening the observatory is open and skies are clear. The Zeiss telescope on the roof is generally open from 7:00pm to 9:45pm.

On Saturday or Sunday, take the **Red Line from Union Station.** If you have come by Metrolink, just tap your ticket at the gate. **Get off at the Vermont/Sunset Station.** You will exit onto Vermont.

1) Background information for Adventure 9 was provided by the observatory and *Los Angeles: An Architectural Guide* by Gebhard and Winter.

The Griffith Observatory

2800 Observatory Road

213-473-0800

Free General Admission

Tuesday–Friday: 12:00noon–10:00pm

Saturday–Sunday: 10:00am–10:00pm • Closed Mondays

Planetarium Theater Shows

Adults: $7 • Seniors and Youth 14–17: $5 • Children 5–12: $3

(Children under five are not admitted to the shows.)

The bus stop for the **Dash Bus Observatory Shuttle** will be in front of you (slightly to your right) on Vermont Avenue as you exit the station. Shuttle service runs from 10:00am to 9:40pm. It is **free** with your Metrolink ticket. After making a few local stops, the shuttle enters Griffith Park and climbs up to the observatory. The trip takes about twenty-five minutes.

Gorgeous light filters through the observatory's lobby entrance doors.

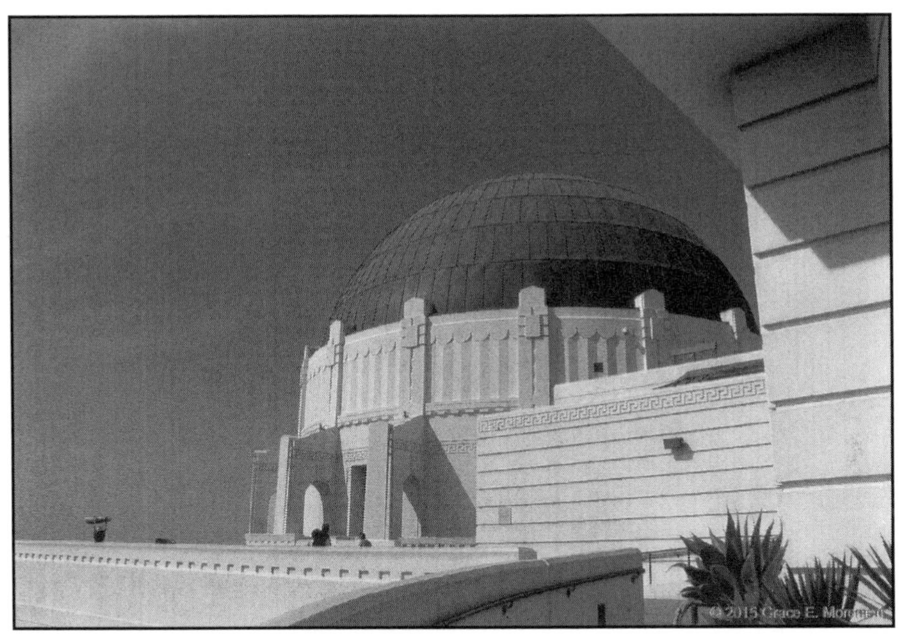

The observatory's dome on the outside balcony with its stunning vistas.

As you enter the lobby, the information desk is on your right, and the ticket desk for the **Planetarium Theater** shows is on your left. **Shows are presented in the Planetarium Theater throughout the day and last thirty** minutes. **Restrooms** are located on either side of the lobby and on the lower level. An elevator is available.

There is a **café** on the lower level with tables inside and out. If you bring your own picnic, you can spread a blanket on the front lawn or sit on one of the benches nearby. A **gift shop** is located near the café.

Come and spend an informative and delightful day at one of LA's most outstanding landmarks. The shows are excellent and will transport you into the heavens. And, if you linger after sunset, you will see the city's famous carpet of lights spread out before you as far as the eye can see.

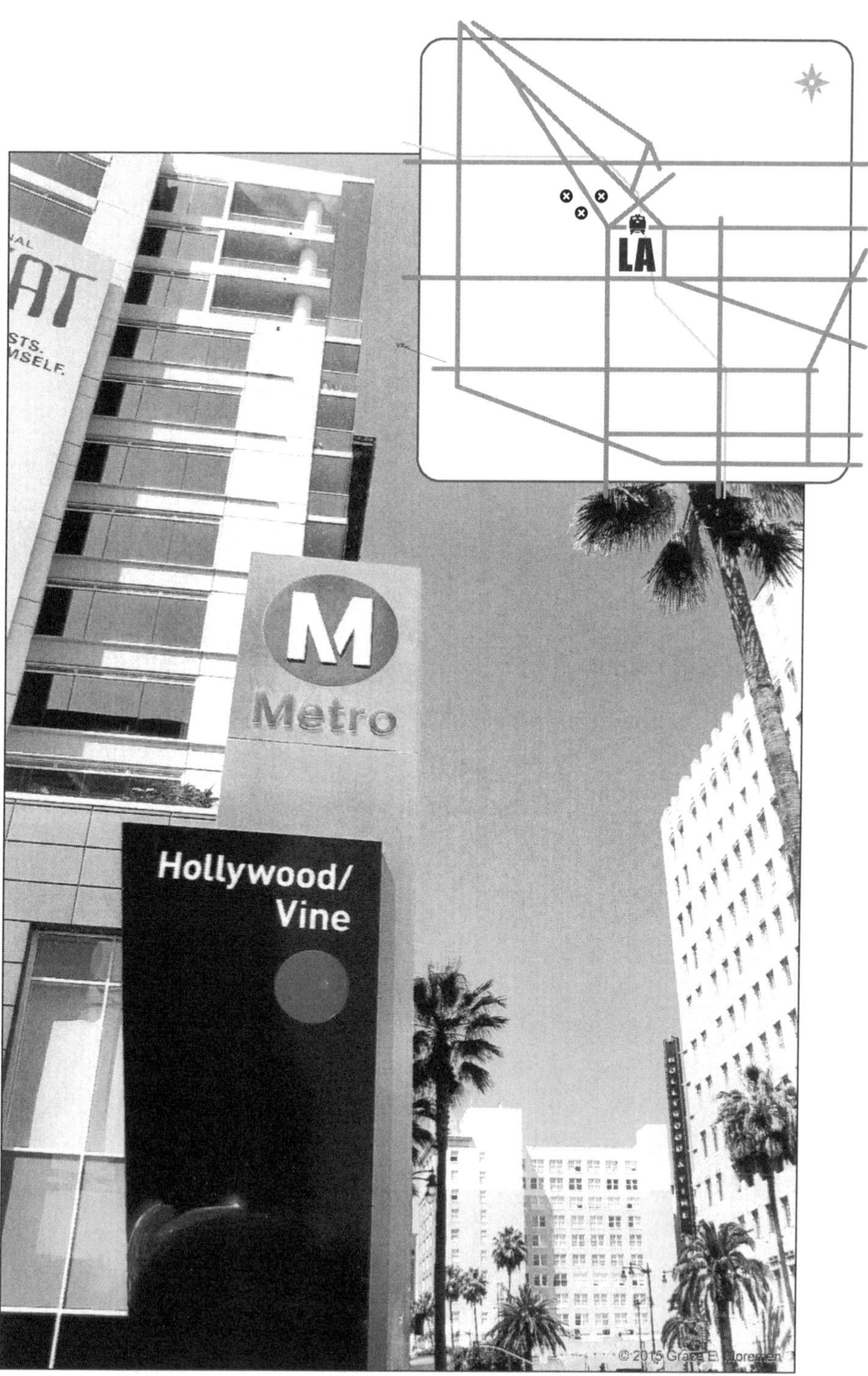
LA
M
Metro
Hollywood/
Vine

All that Glitters

Hollywood • Paramount Pictures and Barnsdall Park

To experience the colorful history of the movies and movie stars, take an Adventure trip to Hollywood. And an early start is recommended! Bring a sandwich or buy one at Union Station before heading off, or plan to stop for a restaurant meal.

 *2 miles minimum*  *8–10 hours*  *varies widely*

What would LA be without **Hollywood**? Their histories are closely entwined.[1] For much of the twentieth century and into the twenty-first, LA has been a "company" town, the "company" being not only the movies, but also a major part of the entire entertainment industry. The motion picture industry was just getting started in 1913 when the Owens River Aqueduct reached the city limits, and LA's population exploded. It was around this time that movie theaters began to proliferate on Broadway in downtown Los Angeles, including **Sid Grauman's Million Dollar Theater** (1918), LA's first grand movie palace. And for the next decade or more, this district ruled as the world's center for the silent silver screen. Sidney Patrick Grauman (1879–1950) was the son of vaudeville performers. He and his father opened their first vaudeville theater in San Francisco around 1900. Sid Grauman moved to Los Angeles in 1917.

1) Background information for Adventure 10 was provided by Red Line Walking Tours and *Los Angeles: An Architectural Guide*, by Gebhard and Winter.

In 1921, real estate developer **Charles E. Toberman** (1880–1981, known as "Mr. Hollywood") persuaded Grauman to build another theater, "The Egyptian," in a brand-new neighborhood called "Hollywoodland." Soon shortened to "Hollywood," the name would become synonymous with America's film industry.

Take the Red Line and exit at Highland. You are now on Hollywood Boulevard, center of "Tinsel Town's" craziness: movie character impersonators, mimes, photo sharks, touts for tours, and the iconic theatres. One of the first things to be noticed: the pink terrazzo stars imbedded in the pavement under your feet that bear the names of Hollywood's greats. This is the famous **Walk of Fame** that extends for blocks along the boulevard. Walking west, on your right, you will see the entrance to the **Hollywood-Highland Center** (2001), a four-story outdoor mall. Take the escalator to the third or fourth level.

As you go up, look above your head to see the gigantic recreations of motifs used in **D.W. Griffith's** silent movie blockbuster, *Intolerance* (1916).

On the walkway under the huge arch you will have a good view of the **Hollywood Sign** (1923) in the distance, perched on the side of Mt. Lee, said to be the most famous and recognizable sign in the world. **Restrooms are located on the second level of the center,** and the **Visitors Information Center** is nearby.

Back on the boulevard, continue walking west and you will come to the entrance of the **Dolby Theater**, where the Academy Awards (Oscars) are held with its famous Red Carpet. You may walk into the lobby and up the broad staircase where the stars have gone before you in anticipation of their big night.

Tours are available. Check the billboard in the lobby for times.

CHINESE THEATRE

TCL Chinese Theater

6925 Hollywood Boulevard

Adjacent to the Dolby Theater is the most famous landmark on Hollywood boulevard: the **TCL Chinese Theater** (1927), **Sid Grauman's** second theater project in Hollywood. Embedded in the cement of the forecourt are the autographs, handprints and footprints of some of the greatest stars: silent film actress Mary Pickford; dancer Fred Astaire; child star Shirley Temple; singing cowboy Roy Rogers and his horse "Trigger;" the Oscars' first African American female host, Whoopi Goldberg, and many, many more.

El Capitan Theater

6838 Hollywood Boulevard

After visiting the Chinese Theater, cross the boulevard, turn left and walk east to continue your promenade along the Walk of Fame. You can't miss the gaudy **El Capitan Theater** which began its life in the vaudeville era. **Judy Garland** and her sisters performed on its stage. It wasn't until 1941 that movies were shown here, beginning with the premiere of *Citizen Kane.* Don't miss the ceiling of the box office lobby and its lavish decoration.

Egyptian Theater

6712 Hollywood Boulevard

When you come to the **Egyptian Theater**, walk around the courtyard and observe the finely painted murals in the ancient Egyptian style. As noted above, this was Hollywood's first movie palace, and when it opened in 1922, King Tutankhamen's ("King Tut's") Tomb had just been discovered, and all things Egyptian became very much in vogue.

Egyptian Theater

As you continue your walk, notice the different logos on the stars in the pavement. They represent five kinds of performance: film, radio, television, stage, and recording. Some performers have more than one star on the boulevard, signifying that they excelled in more than one medium. **At the corner of Hollywood and Vine there is a Starbuck's. It's not a bad place to enjoy watching the world of Hollywood Boulevard go by, and it has a Restroom.** If you would like to eat in a restaurant, you might want to try **Musso & Frank Grill,** established in 1919, located at 6667 Hollywood Blvd. American menu, $7–$30. **Reservations suggested, 323-467-5132;** or **Delphine Eatery & Bar,** 6250 Hollywood Blvd. **323-798-1355** Mediterranean menu, $13–$37.

The Metro station is just a little farther east. Opposite the station across the boulevard is the **Pantages Theater** (1930), an *Art Deco*-style movie palace where the Academy Awards were held from 1949 to 1959. Today, live performances of musicals and dance are presented there.

Hollywood and Vine Metro Station

The **Hollywood and Vine Metro Station** (1999) is full of delightful movie-related décor, including colorful tile murals, film projectors, old movie reels that line the ceiling, and stylized, stage-lit palm trees. Take a few minutes to enjoy it all before you head back to Union Station.

There are two additional choices for your day in Hollywood:

1) Take a behind-the-scenes tour of Paramount Pictures Studio located at **5555 Melrose Avenue.** You will see segments from movies and TV shows, such as the bench in *Forrest Gump*; a New York street from the TV series *Seinfeld*; the windows of Lucille Ball's office during the *I Love Lucy* years; and sets for current TV shows. You will also see a how an "ocean" is created. Paramount is the last remaining major studio in Hollywood. It is accessible on the **#210 Local orange bus** that runs north and south on Vine Street. **Catch it on the southwest corner of Hollywood and Vine for the short ride**. At Melrose get off and walk two blocks east to the entrance of the studio.

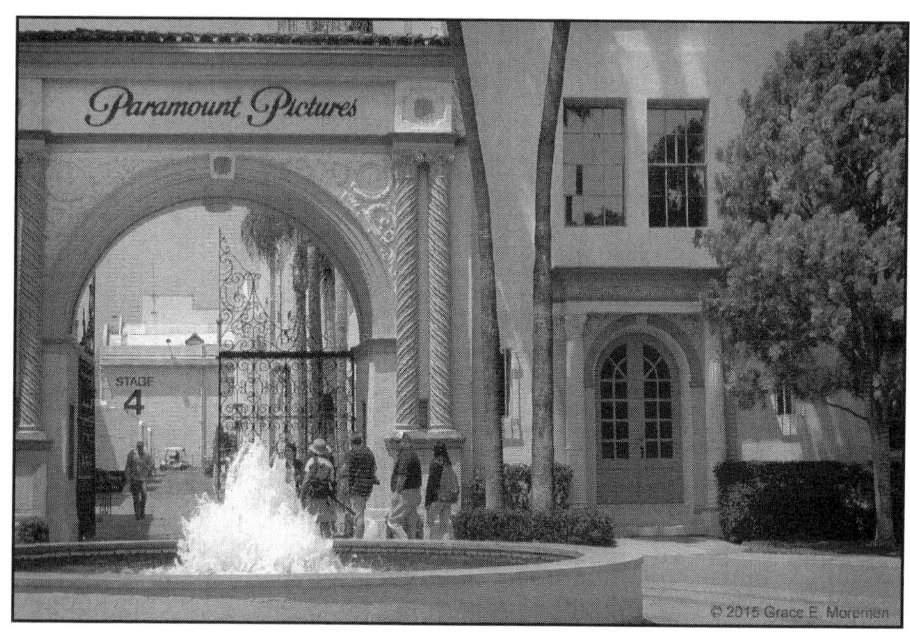

Paramount Pictures

5555 Melrose Avenue

323-956-5000 • www.paramountstudiotour.com

2-hour Tram Tour: $53 (age 10 and above only)

Advance reservations necessary

After the tour catch the **#210 Local bus (marked "Hollywood and Vine")** on the **southeast corner of Vine and Melrose, for the return to Hollywood Boulevard and the Red Line Station.**

2) Another must-see in Hollywood is Barnsdall Park. Located about a mile east of Hollywood and Vine **at 4800 Hollywood Boulevard,** Barnsdall Park is crowned by a masterpiece, a home designed by **Frank Lloyd Wright** (1867–1959).

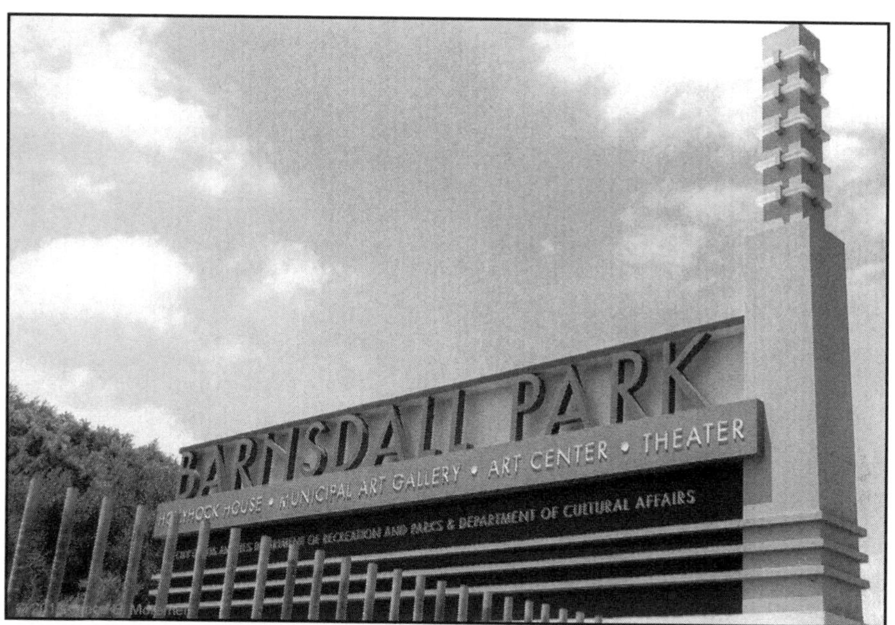

Barnsdall Park

4800 Hollywood Boulevard

323-644-6269 • barnsdall.org/visit/

Municipal Art Gallery: Thursday–Sunday • 12noon to 5:00pm

Hollyhock House: Thursday–Sunday • 11:00am–3:00pm

To reach it, catch the #180 local eastbound bus at Hollywood Boulevard and Argyle Street for a ten minute ride. Exit at Hollywood Blvd. and Prospect Street. *(Prospect becomes Hollywood Blvd.)* **Walk back** ***(west)*** **one block to the Barnsdall Park entrance.**

Either road or stairs will lead you up **Olive Hill**, a surprising, free-standing promontory in the midst of Hollywood. At the top, you will see several sand-colored buildings, all in *Mayan Revival*-style. The buildings' clean lines and restrained decoration are typical of Frank Lloyd Wright. **Rudolph Schindler** (1887–1953) and **Richard Neutra** (1892–1970), protégés of Wright, as well as Wright's son,

Hollyhock House

323-913-4031 • www.barnsdall.org/visit/hollyhock-house/tours/

Hours: Thursday–Sunday • 11:00am–3:00pm

General Admission: $7

Students/Seniors with valid ID: $3

Children 12 and under (with paying adult): $3

Tickets sold onsite by Credit Card only.

Lloyd Wright (1890–1978), also worked on these buildings. All became trend-setting architects in Southern California.

The main structure, ***Hollyhock House***, is named for the favorite flower of **Aline Barnsdall**, who commissioned the house. The walls and roofline are embellished with stylized hollyhocks, which are repeated elsewhere on the estate.

Having inherited a fortune from her father, Aline Barnsdall moved to Hollywood from Pennsylvania in 1917, and purchased the 35-acre Olive Hill property. She hired Wright to design her house as a place for the "progressive theatrical community" to gather.

Built between 1919 and 1923 it was Wright's first commission in Los Angeles. A dedicated patron of the arts, Ms. Barnsdall not only supported avant-garde architects, she was also a promoter of the development of the **Hollywood Bowl.**

In 1926, Aline Barnsdall gave her Olive Hill estate to the City of Los Angeles to be used as a cultural center, although she continued to live in the house until her death in 1946. Today the eleven-acre park, maintained by the Cultural Affairs Department of the City of Los Angeles, also contains an arts center and a performance theater.

Take some time to enjoy the spacious, **360-degree view of Hollywood, including the Griffith Observatory and the Hollywood Sign.** Don't forget to walk around to the east side of the Hollyhock House to see the ornamental pool and inner courtyard. **Restrooms** are located in the lobby of the theater building.

Hollyhock House is on the National Register of Historic Places, is a U.S. National Historic Landmark, and also ranks as Los Angeles Historic-Cultural Monument #12. After being completely renovated, the **interior of the house** was re-opened to the public in February 2015.

To exit the park, walk south on the grounds (away from Hollywood Blvd.) **and find the stairs.** Notice the colorful murals painted by children on the walls of the Junior Arts center. The stairs will take you down to Vermont Avenue. **Cross Vermont Avenue; the Metro station will be a short distance on your right. Take the Red Line back to Union Station.**

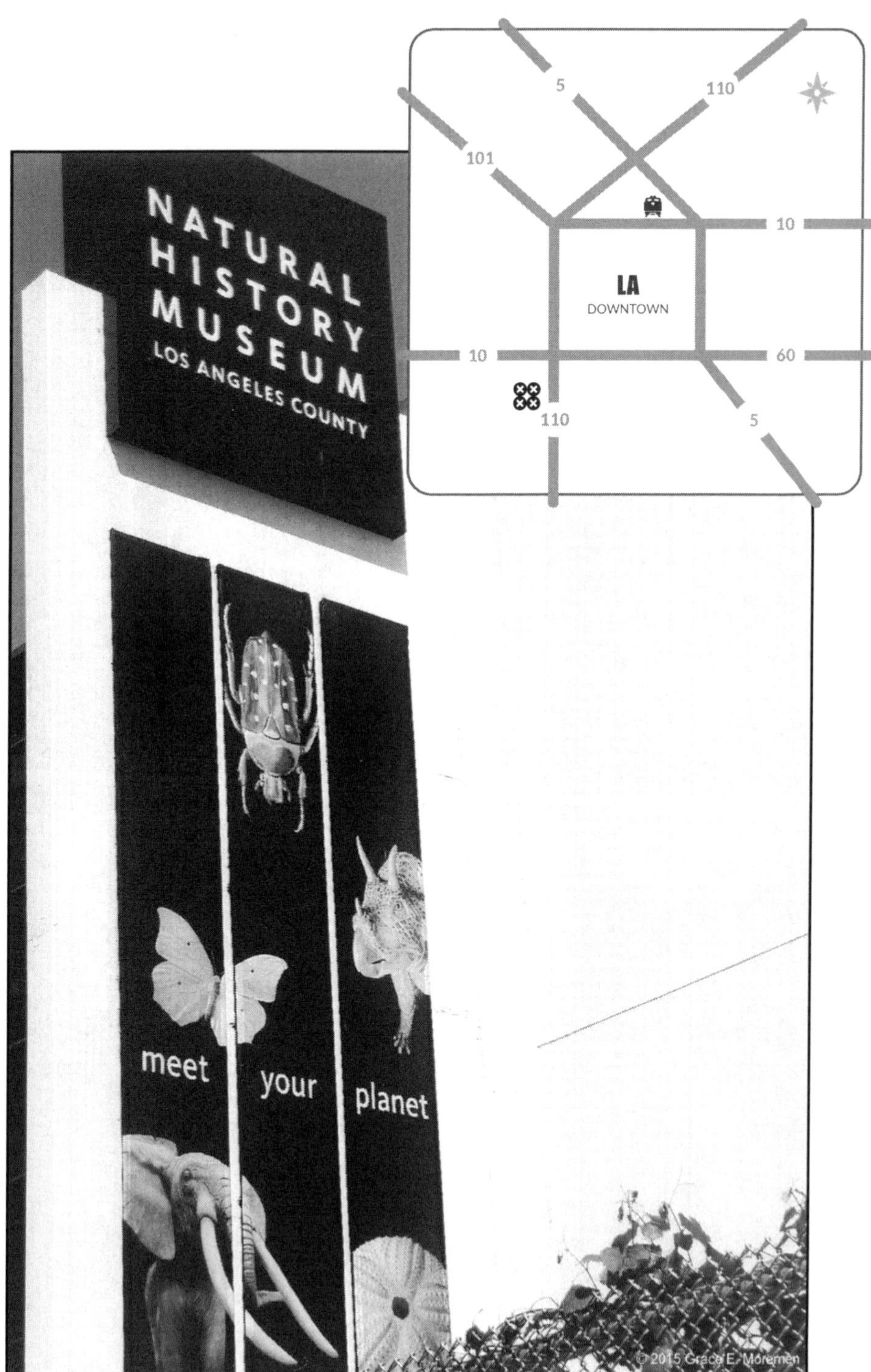
NATURAL HISTORY MUSEUM
LOS ANGELES COUNTY
meet
your
planet
© 2015 Grace E. Moremen
5
110
101
10
LA
DOWNTOWN
10
60
110
5

Exuberant Exposition Park: 3 Amazing Museums & a Rose Garden

California Science Center and IMAX Theater
Museum of Natural History • Rose Garden
California African American Museum

 *2 miles max?*  *4–6 hours*  *minimum*

Located just south of downtown, Exposition Park is one of the city's greatest cultural resources. Home to the august ***Los Angeles Coliseum****, site of the 1932 and 1984 Summer Olympic Games, Exposition Park also boasts three world-class must-see museums: the California Science Center, permanent home of the space shuttle* ***Endeavour****; the Museum of Natural History of LA County; and the California African-American Museum. Flanking the museums is the magnificent seven-acre sunken Rose Garden.*[1] *The 162-acre Exposition Park belongs to the State of California and dates from 1872, when it opened as a fairground. The park stands directly opposite the campus of the* ***University of Southern California (USC).***[2]

1) Unless otherwise indicated, information for Adventure 11 was provided by the museums.
2) Founded in 1880, USC was one of the earliest institutions of higher learning established in Southern California.

Exposition Park

700 Exposition Park Drive

323-724-3623 • californiasciencecenter.org/imax

Open: Daily 10:00am–5:00pm

Closed: Thanksgiving, Christmas, and New Year's Day

Free General Admission • Cost for Imax Theater and Endeavour

Rose Garden Plaza

Hours: 9:00am–6:00pm

Free admission

Closed January to March (*for pruning*)

Cross Exposition Boulevard and enter the park. You will be in the famous **Rose Garden**, which has been enjoyed by Angelenos since 1928. A sunken garden of seven acres, it is home to 15,000 rosebushes, in over 100 varieties, and has been on the National Register of Historic Places since 1991. It is worth taking some time to slow down, walk among the roses and enjoy the expanse of color and fragrance.

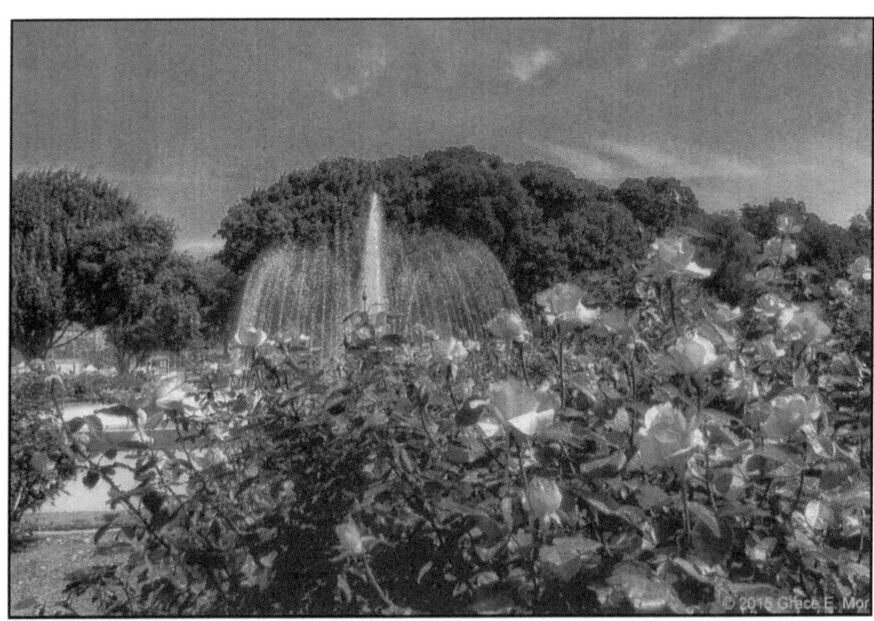

11

California Science Center and IMAX Theater

700 Exposition Park Drive

323-724-3623 • californiasciencecenter.org/imax

Open Daily 10:00am–5:00pm

Closed Thanksgiving, Christmas, and New Year's Day

Free General Admission • Cost for Imax Theater and *Endeavour*

Proceed through the Rose Garden, past the beautiful fountain, and straight up the stairs to the **California Science Center**. Opened in **1998**, with its 400,000 square feet of exhibition space, this museum is touted as "the West Coast's largest hands-on science center." Its mission is "to stimulate curiosity and inspire science learning in everyone." On any given weekday the museum will be bustling with school children and their teachers, many wearing colorful school shirts. They will be everywhere, interacting in each of the exhibition areas: **Ecosystems, World of Life, Creative World, Air and Space,** and of course **the Space Shuttle *Endeavour*.**

Enormous and majestic, the *Endeavour* was installed in its own quarters, the **Samuel Oschin Pavilion**, in **2012**.[1] On your way to see it, ride the escalator up to the second floor and experience the preview of *Endeavour: The California Story*, followed by a film about the *Endeavour's* journey back to its birthplace in Southern California, its dramatic landing at Edwards Air Force Base atop a 747 jet plane, and the breathtaking scenes of its two-day journey on October 12 and 13, 2012 through the people-lined streets of LA.[2]

To reach the *Endeavour*, ride the elevator down to the first floor and enter the large structure where it is housed. The gigantic scale of this spacecraft is overwhelming. Don't be surprised if you feel greatly moved

---

1) Samuel Oschin (1914–2003) was a Los Angeles entrepreneur and philanthropist.

2) One incredibly tight turn occurred in Inglewood, just two blocks from where Grace once lived. Pretty exciting.

to stand in its presence. It is a real treasure, having traveled 123 million miles through outer space in order to complete its 25 missions. Well-informed docents are on duty to answer your questions.

Exit the California Science Center by the way you entered, turn left, and proceed to the **Museum of Natural History.** Notice the older building that adjoins the main building (at right). Completed in **1913**, it was designed by the architects **Frank Hudson** and **William A. D. Munsell.** This century-old building is a pleasant blending of the *Spanish Renaissance*-style with *Beaux Arts.*

As you enter the museum you are in the new **Dinosaur Hall** with over 300 fossils and 20 complete dinosaurs and ancient sea creatures. Here you will have the rare opportunity of seeing *T. Rex* in three different growth stages of its life: baby, juvenile, and sub-adult. These creatures lived an astounding 66 million years ago and were collected in Garfield County, Montana in the late 1960s.[3] Enjoy the close-up fossils in this exhibition. There are also many hands-on, multimedia stations to explore. For example, you can watch a dinosaur hunting expedition.

---

3) www.nhm.org/site/sites/default/files/pdf/press/recent/2011_trexseries.pdf

11

Museum of Natural History

900 Exposition Boulevard

213-763-3426 • nhm.org

Open Daily 9:30am–5:30pm

General Admission: $12 • Seniors 62+: $9 • Students: $9

Children 3-12: $5 • Age 2 and under: Free

For visiting exhibits there is an additional fee.

Proceed to the 1913 ***Beaux Arts*** wing, the original part of the museum. The spacious, elegant rotunda measures 75 feet across with three extending wings. Notice the Italian marble walls and the mosaic tile floor. Central to the room is the signature statue of the ***Three Muses*** by American sculptor **Julia Bracken Wendt** (1870–1942). Overhead, a dome soars up 58 feet to a skylight 20 feet across created by **Walter Horace Judson**, of the Judson Studios, specialists in fine arts stained glass. Go up to the second floor and get a bird's eye view of the *Three Muses* below.[4] The mission of the Natural History Museum of Los Angeles is "to inspire wonder, discovery and responsibility for our

4) nhm.org/site/about-our-museums/history

natural and cultural worlds." Other popular exhibits are the **Insect Zoo** and the beautiful dioramas of **African Mammals** and **North American Mammals.** The museum also regularly hosts visiting exhibitions.

Some of the museum's special highlights are **LA Meteorite, Fin Whale,** and **LA City Model: *Becoming Los Angeles*.** In addition there are **"Hidden Gems,"** special plants and animals hidden in plain sight throughout the museum, such as a **Pregnant Plesiosaur**, a **Listening Tree**, and a **Live Newt**—a few more things to keep you exploring.

If it's lunchtime, the **NHM Grill** offers made-to-order hot food, or you can enjoy your own picnic on the **South Lawn** or in the **Amphitheater.**

Exit the NHM through the main entrance. Before you is the **LA Coliseum.** Completed in 1923, it is the home of the USC Trojans football team and a major sports and special events venue, with a current seating capacity of 93,607. The LA Coliseum is the only facility in the world to have hosted two Olympic Games. It is another example of the work of architects **John and Donald Parkinson.**

Walk left, past the California Science Center and shortly you will come to the **California African American Museum.**

11

California African American

600 State Drive

213-744-7432 • caamuseum.org

Tuesday–Saturday 10:00am–5:00pm

Sunday 11:00am–5:00pm • Closed Monday

Free Admission

At the entry is a captivating metal sculpture, ***Wishing On a Star***, a human figure fashioned from recycled materials by African Diaspora sculptor **Charles Dickson.**[5] You may spy a Dell computer, a carburetor, a funnel, socket wrenches and, of course, "rebar" (steel rods used to reinforce concrete). Enter the glass-covered forecourt of the museum, a spacious and light-filled room. This building encompasses 44,000 square feet, including three full-size exhibition galleries, a conference center, and a research library.

Wikimedia courtesy Jlim06 © 2014

5) roadsideamerica.com/tip/31799

© 2015 Grace E. Moremen

The mission of the museum is "to research, collect, preserve, and interpret for public enrichment the history, art and culture of African Americans with an emphasis on California and the western United States." The museum was chartered by the State of California in 1977, opened in 1981 in temporary quarters, and relocated to its present site in 1984. African American architects **Jack Haywood** and the late **Vince Proby** designed the building.

The research library has over 20,000 items, including an 1855 edition of *My Bondage and My Freedom* by **Frederick Douglass** (c.1818–1895) and books by, for example, **Zora Neale Hurston** (1891–1960), **Maya Angelou** (1928–2014), and **Langston Hughes** (1902–1967). The library also owns older issues of the African American newspapers *Chicago Defender* and the *Pittsburgh Courier.*

At any given time, the museum may be hosting as many as six traveling exhibitions. Its permanent collection includes **Academic and Naturalistic Landscape Painting of the Nineteenth Century, Modern and Contemporary Art, Contemporary Art from the African Diaspora,** and **Traditional African Art.**

To return to Union Station, **go back to the Expo Line Station.** Take the **train marked "Downtown."** Exit at the **Seventh Street/ Metro Center Station.** Go downstairs, and **catch the train marked "Union Station."**

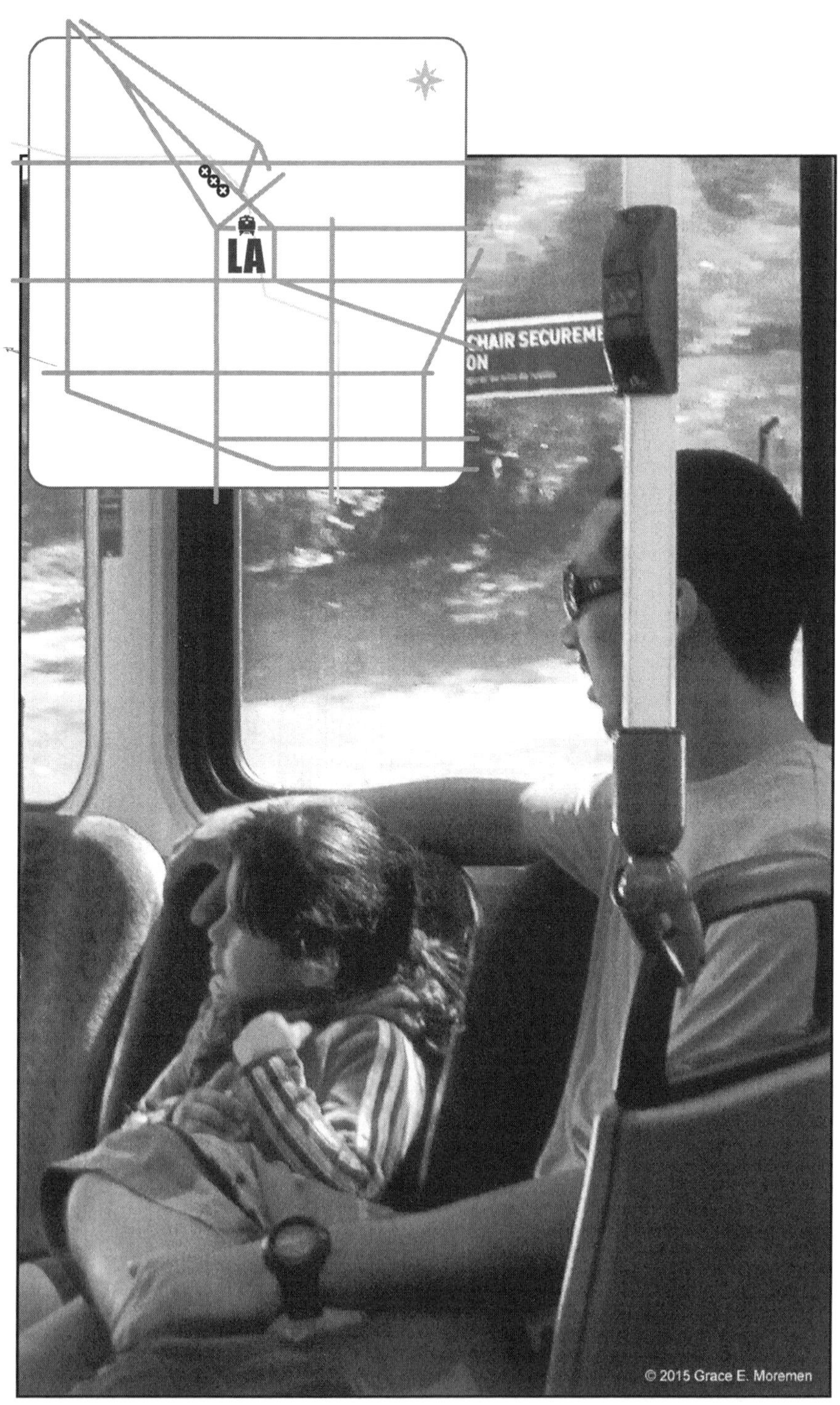
LA
CHAIR SECUREME
ON
© 2015 Grace E. Moremen

12

Griffith Park: Something for Everyone

Los Angeles Zoo and Botanical Gardens
The Autry National Center
Pony Rides and Miniature Train

This Adventure covers a good deal of territory, so you may have to choose one or two places. But it is a lot of fun to ride the bus to and through the park, which is free with your Metrolink Ticket.

 *2 miles max*  *7-9 hours* 

all four fees

These Adventures would not be complete without a visit to **Griffith Park.** Los Angeles is greatly blessed to have one of the largest urban parks in the country that covers over 94,310 acres of riverside and mountainous terrain. Once part of the Los Feliz Rancho, the land was given to the city in 1896 by **Colonel Griffith J. Griffith** (1850–1919), who made his fortune in mining. Well supplied with hiking and biking trails, today the park sports three golf courses, numerous playing fields, an **Observatory** (see Adventure 9), and the **Greek Theater,** a major outdoor stage for the performing arts.

Among the park's finest attractions are the **Los Angeles Zoo and**

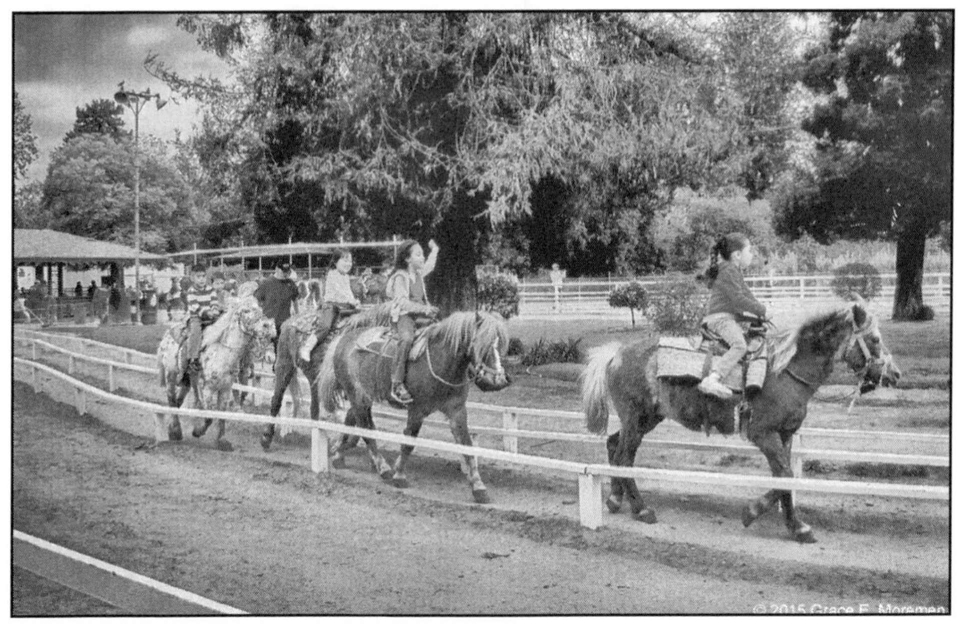

Botanical Gardens, the **Autry National Center,** and a venue for **pony rides** and a **miniature train.** These places are located on the eastern, flat portion of the park that borders the LA River. All are accessible by public transportation.

Pack a picnic lunch or buy a sandwich, and get an early start. Before you leave **pick up a schedule for MTA Local #96 bus at the east end of Union Station.**

Take the Metro **Red or Purple Line one stop to Civic Center Station. Exit to First Street. Catch the #96 bus** on the southwest corner of First and Hill Streets (that's around to your left as you come out of the Metro Station). The bus's **destination** will be marked **"Burbank Station."** It takes about forty minutes to reach the zoo. The ride is enjoyable and interesting, and it will give you a chance to see some of this fabulous park.

A short time before reaching the zoo, the bus driver will announce "**pony rides**." One of the oldest attractions still operating in the park, pony rides have been in existence for over sixty years! The **miniature**

12

Pony Rides and Miniature Train

4400 Crystal Springs Drive

323-664-3266

Tuesday–Sunday: 10:00am–4:00pm

$3 for a five-minute pony ride • Train: $2.75 for all ages

train is located in the same area. If you have very young children, this may be the destination for you. Before you get off, ask the driver how often the buses run so you will have an idea when the next bus can be expected.

The well-supervised pony rides last about five minutes and are very popular with children. The one mile train ride lasts eight or nine minutes and the adults enjoy it as much as the youngsters. There is a snack bar with picnic tables, and **Restrooms** are available.. **If you want to continue to the Zoo/and or the Autry, stay on the bus.**

The zoo is about three miles farther along the road. As you get off the bus, note the time, and ask the driver how often the buses run, so you will have an idea of when to return. You can also check your **#96 bus schedule.**

Los Angeles Zoo and Botanical Gardens

5333 Zoo Drive

323-644-4200 • lazoo.tickets@lacity.org

Hours: Daily 10:45am–4:45pm

Adults age 13 up: $18 • Seniors: $15 • Children age 2–12: $13

Founded in 1966, the **LA Zoo and Botanical Gardens** complex covers 331 acres, and is home to lions, tigers, elephants, chimpanzees, koalas, hedgehogs, birds, reptiles and amphibians, in fact, over 1000 different species. Notice and enjoy the botanical plantings as you stroll the grounds. The plants provide food and habitat for the animals. This is an extremely child-friendly place with many activities for all ages. There are food concessions, or you can bring your own picnic.

Restrooms are available.

It is a short walk across the road to the **Autry National Center,** a museum of the American West established in 1988. Don't miss the dramatic, life-size bronze sculpture out in front, by American painter

The Autry National Center

4700 Western Heritage Way

323-667-2000 • theautry.org

Tuesday–Friday: 10am–4pm • Saturday & Sunday: 10am–5pm

Closed Monday and major holidays*

Adults: $10 • Students & Seniors (60+): $6 • Children (3–12): $4

and sculptor **Douglas van Howd** that captures the dramatic moment of transference of a mail bag to a galloping pony express rider. The fast action is highlighted by the flying fringe on the rider's jacket. This outstanding sculpure was ranked 63 out of 1,052 attractions in Los Angeles. In the courtyard you will see a bronze statue by local artist **David L. Spellerberg** that honors **Gene Autry** (1907–1998), film star, "singing cowboy," and founder of the center. In 2003 the Autry National Center merged with the Southwest Museum of the American Indian and was blessed with that museum's stellar collection of baskets, pottery, and other Indian artifacts, numbering over 237,000 items. As noted in Adventure 18, the Southwest Museum was founded in 1913 and its venerable building sits on the southern slope of Mount Washington in the Highland Park District of Los Angeles. Grace fondly remembers visiting it on a school field trip in the 1940s. Over the years the Southwest Museum was damaged by earthquakes and developed financial difficulties. The merger brought LA's oldest museum together with one of the newest, which was beneficial to both. Check the Autry Center's website for current exhibitions.

You don't have to enter the museum to enjoy the patio, which is a pleasant place to relax and have your picnic. There is also a café. **Restrooms** are located nearby.

For your return, **go to the same bus stop** where you exited the **#96 bus.** The southbound bus will be marked **"Downtown."** Exit the bus at **Civic Center Metro Station at First and Hill Streets,** and take the **subway back to Union Station.**

* except Martin Luther King Day and Presidents Day when admission is free.

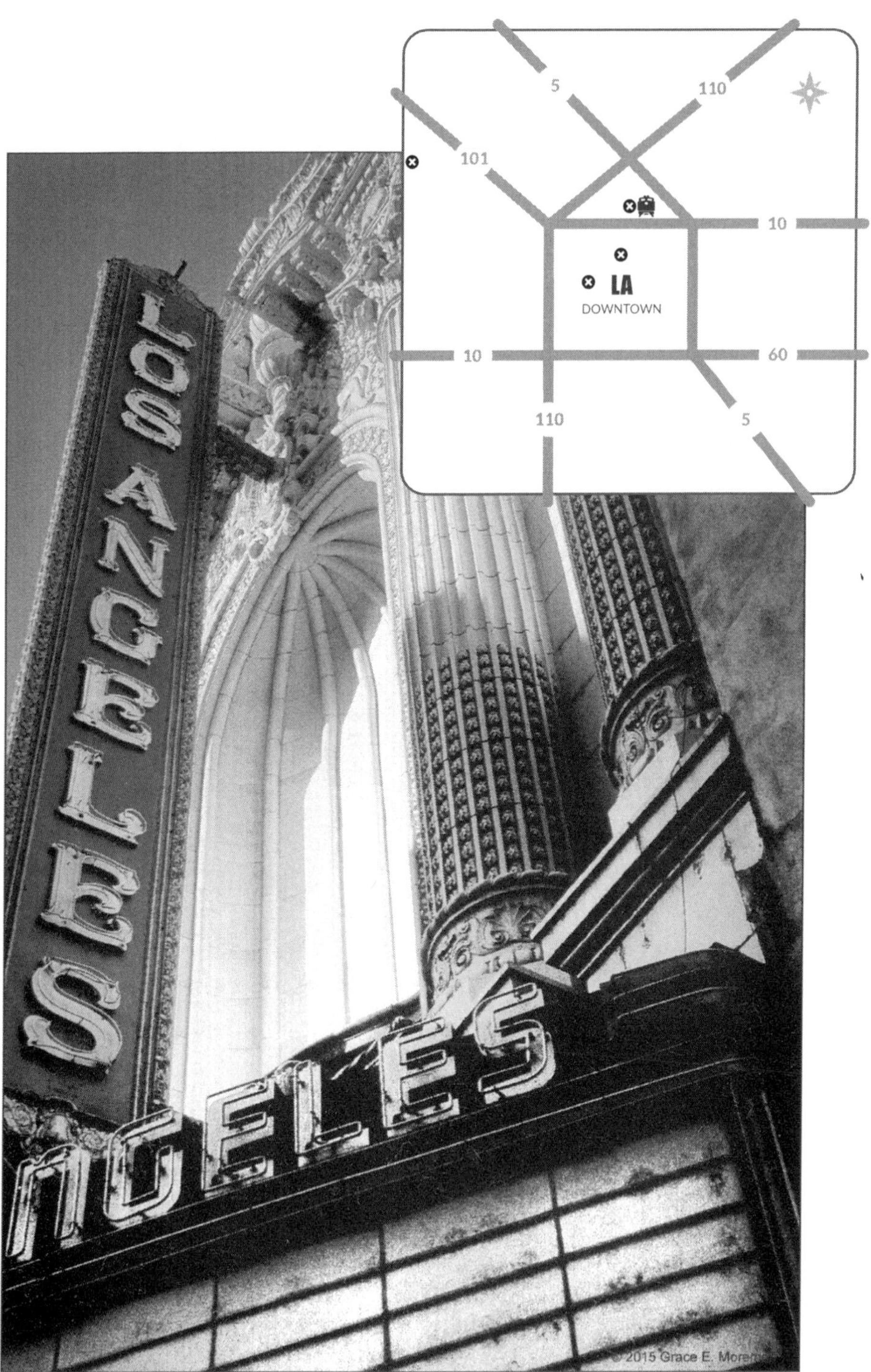
5
110
101
10
LA
DOWNTOWN
10
60
110
5
LOS ANGELES
© 2015 Grace E. Moren

13

Touring with the Pros

LA Conservancy Walking Tours
The Neon Cruise • Metro Art Tours

The modes of transportation and the distances vary from tour to tour. These tours are sponsored by non-profit organizations. We have participated in all of them and highly recommend all three. The Metro Art Tour is free. Proceeds from the the LA Conservancy and The Neon Cruise benefit their respective organizations.

The Neon Cruise is, perhaps, the most unusual Los Angeles event we have ever experienced, and perhaps the most fun! You tour downtown LA and Hollywood on a summer's night on top of a double-decker bus.

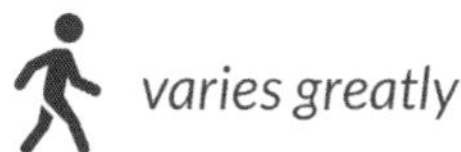
varies greatly

2–4 hours

see tours

GIFTS
© 2015 Grace E. Moremen
Canters
RESTAURANT
BAKERY
© 2015 Grace E. Moremen

13

    *Steep stairs to top of double-decker bus, otherwise very little walking*

The Neon Cruise

sponsored by the Museum of Neon Art

213-489-9918 • neonmona.org

Cost: $55 • $45 for MONA members

Saturdays: June–September

Double-decker bus departs at 7:00pm

(in downtown LA at a specified location)

Sponsored by the **Museum of Neon Art** and conducted by a personable and knowledgeable docent, you climb to the top level of the bus and "cruise" for the next two and a half hours taking note of the brilliant, and unexpectedly varied and beautiful, neon signage along the way. Wine and/or water are offered and soon you are immersed in a panoply of darkness and light, with the night breeze blowing on your face. As a student in an English-as-a-Second-Language class once wrote: [*Driving at night in LA*] "makes me having my best delightful ...It's to enjoy the two light streams [of traffic], one is red and another is white. They flow stoplessly in the opposition directions to the infinitive horizon."[1]

The Neon Cruise might prove to be one of your "best delightfuls!"

Check their website for information and to make your reservation.

1) Jack Smith, *Alive in LaLa Land.* Franklin Watts, *1989,* page 6.

The soaring interior of the Los Angeles Theater

   *2 miles max for most tours*

LA Conservancy Walking Tours

213-623-2489 • laconservancy.com

Cost: $10 • $5 for members

Saturdays 10:00am • most tours start at Pershing Square

This heroic organization was founded in 1978 during a time of crisis in Los Angeles. The **Central Library** had outgrown its space and there was serious talk of moving it to the San Fernando Valley. In addition, two arson fires greatly damaged the building in 1984. The **LA Conservancy** grew out of the group that succeeded in saving this iconic building. Since that time the Conservancy has rescued many other historic sites in the city. They conduct a variety of walking tours of downtown every Saturday morning, starting at 10:00am. Most tours start at **Pershing Square**, easily reached by Metro. There are also some afternoon tours. Go to **LAConservancy.com** for **schedules and locations.**

13

Flying figures at Civic Center Station

    *1½ miles max*

Metro Art Tours

213-922-2738 • metro.net/aboutart

1st Saturday and Sunday of each month

Free

These walking tours are held the first Saturday and Sunday of each month. They are free and last about two hours. One is in **Hollywood** and the other starts in **Union Station**. Knowledgeable guides take you under their capable wings and lead you to see the art in three stations. It is astounding how much art is out there! When you're in a hurry to get somewhere, you probably don't take time to notice the art, at least not in detail.[2] These tours are lots of fun and are very informative. Go to the **website for information about starting times and locations.**

2) For example, we were amazed when the guide told the group to look up and see the flying figures overhead at the Civic Center Station. We had never noticed them, even though we had walked through that station dozens of times.

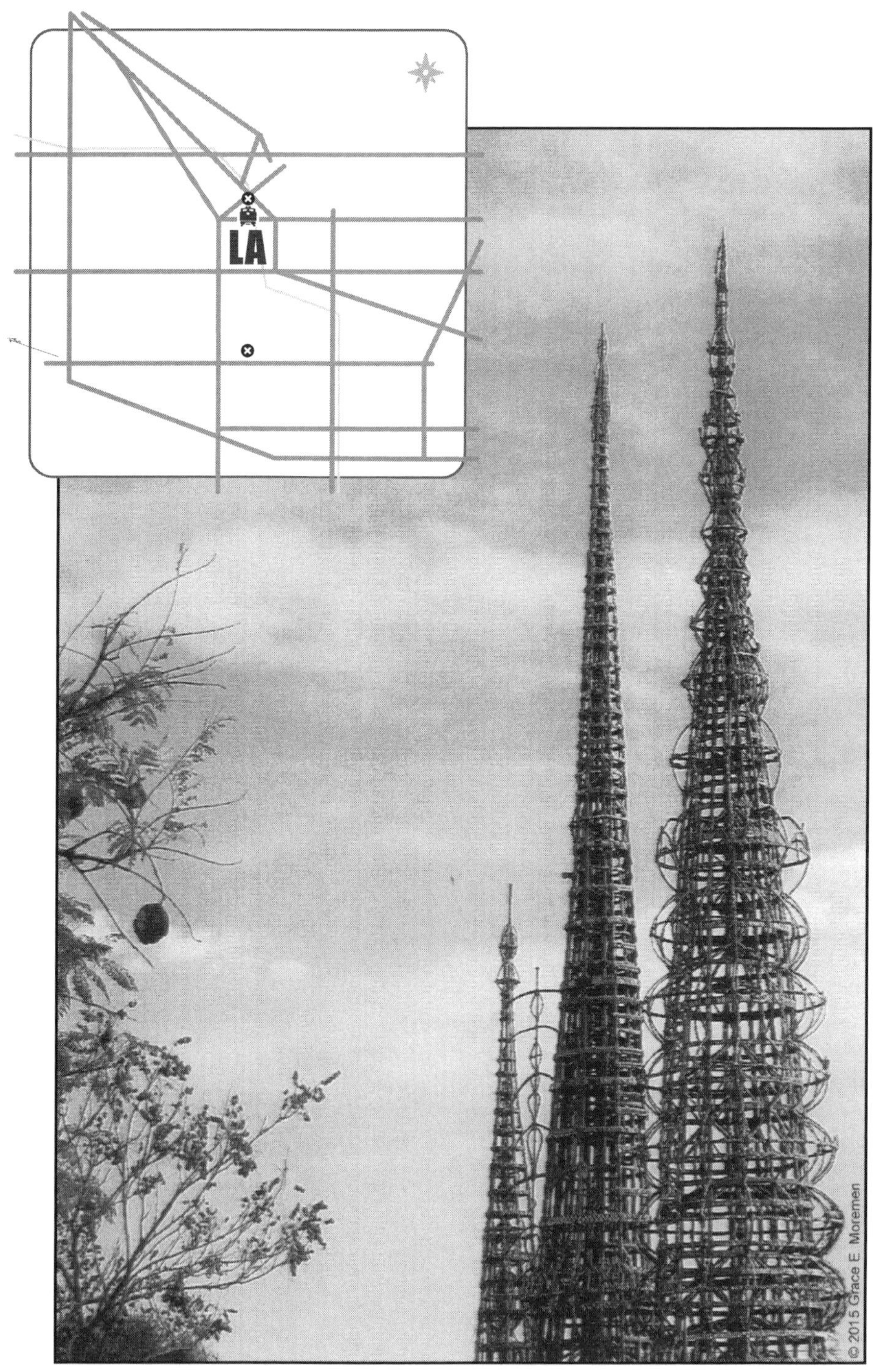
LA
© 2015 Grace E. Moremen

14

The Folly of Simon Rodia:
Watts Towers

Simon Rodia National Historic Park
Homegirl Café & Bakery

These two destinations, though located several miles apart, will gladden your heart. Simon Rodia National Historic Park, better known as Watts Towers, and Homegirl Café & Bakery have valuable qualities in common. Both are monuments to the human spirit and the fruits of a persistent, singular vision. Both are easily accessible by public transportation and are well worth visiting.

 *1½ miles max*  *4–5 hours* 

food & fee

Try to arrive at Union Station by 10:00–10:30 a.m. You can begin this Adventure with a late breakfast or an early lunch at **Homegirl Café and Bakery,** located on Alameda Street three blocks north of Union Station. Walk or **take the Gold Line (direction Sierra Madre) at Union Station. Exit the first stop (Chinatown)** and cross Alameda Street to Homegirl Café. The café and bakery are part of the **Homeboy Industries** complex.[1] The atmosphere is very friendly, the food and service are excellent, and the bakery goods are top quality.[2]

1) Homeboy Industries was founded by Father Gregory Boyle with the goal of "providing hope, training, and support to formerly gang-involved men and women." (HomeBoyIndustries.org)
2) Homegirl Café may be closed on some weekends. Another choice is Philippe's, at 1001 N. Alameda Street, established in 1927 and famous for French dip sandwiches ($7–$10).

Homegirl Café and Bakery

130 West Bruno Street
homeboyindustries.org/
what-we-do/homegirl-cafe/welcome/
323-526-1254

After your meal, return to Union Station and take the **Metro (either Red or Purple Line)** to **Metro Center Station. Walk upstairs, tap your ticket again, and transfer to the Blue Line, direction "Long Beach."**

Exit at the 103rd Street Station. Walk south about three blocks on Graham Avenue (paralleling the tracks). Following Graham Avenue, which will curve to the left past the Methodist Church, you will see the towers in the near distance.

Homegirl Cafe & Bakery

14

Simon Rodia National Historic

1727 E. 107th Street

213-847-4446 • parks.ca.gov/default.asp

Arts Center: Wednesday–Saturday 10:00am–4:00pm •

Sunday 12noon–4:00pm

Admission to the Towers is by guided tour only:

Thursday–Saturday 10:30am–3:00pm • Sunday 12:30pm–3:00pm

Cost: $7 (You can view from the exterior for free.)

This amazing complex of spires and walls was built over a thirty-three year period between 1921 and 1954 by **Sabato** or **"Sam"** or **"Simon" Rodia** (1879–1965).[3] Born in Rivatoli, Italy, a peasant community twenty miles east of Naples, Sam, at age fifteen, immigrated to the United States around 1894. He lived with his brother in Pennsylvania for several years, working as a laborer in construction. After his brother's death, Sam moved to Seattle where he married Lucy Ucci. The couple had three children, one of whom died at a young age. Later they moved to Oakland, California. They were divorced in 1912, and a few years later Sam moved to Southern California. In 1921 he purchased a small house on a pie-shaped lot next to the **Pacific Electric** tracks in the Watts district of Los Angeles. A construction worker by day, at night and on weekends Sam began to create a mysterious project in his backyard. He said he wanted "to build something big," and he succeeded. **The tallest spire is 99.5 feet high!** He also built a wall around the towers with several archway openings—all accomplished without help, without scaffolding or modern equipment. Built of steel and covered with mortar, Rodia embellished it all with colorful bits of glass, seashells, pottery, tile, mirrors, and other such objects. What immediately strikes you is the towers' graceful appearance, their colors, and delightful whimsy. Yet, the structures are substantial. When the city was considering demolishing them in the 1970s, a severe stress test was applied—the towers survived beautifully.

3) Rodia never used the name "Simon," a name that was inaccurately attributed to him in an article in the *Los Angeles Times* in 1937. However, the name stuck.

Where did Rodia get his inspiration for the towers? In Avellino, Italy, near Rodia's hometown, there is an annual harvest festival in late summer where wooden, obelisk-like structures as much as seventy feet high are pulled through the streets on wagons. Dedicated to the Madonna, these processions were witnessed by Rodia as a boy. His curious towers in fact resemble those old-world obelisks.[4] ***Be sure and visit the beautiful exhibits in two galleries***: the **Watts Towers Arts Center** and the **Charles Mingus Youth Arts Center.**[5]

The **Simon Rodia National Historic Park** has been designated a "folk art environment," one of nine listed in the National Register of Historic Places. The property was deeded to the State of California in 1978 as a unit of the State Parks system. It is managed by the **Los Angeles Cultural Affairs Department,** which organizes rotating exhibits and conducts a number of arts-related activities for young people.

Sam Rodia left a remarkable achievement in his adopted country, an inspiring work of art that will amaze you and lift your spirits.

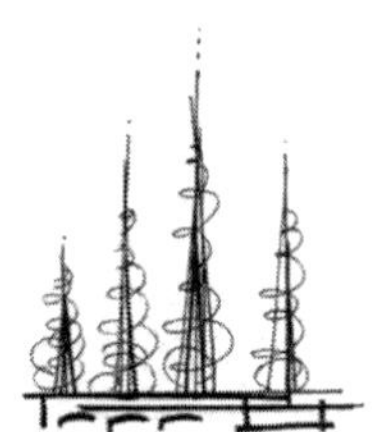

Walk back to the 103rd Street Station and catch the train marked "Downtown Los Angeles." Transfer at Metro Center (downstairs), and take the train back to **Union Station.**

---

4) Information provided by Ms. Rosie Lee Hooks, director of the Watts Towers Cultural Center. When Ms. Hooks visited Avellino, Italy, in 2013, she brought back a small model of one of the towers carried in the procession, which is on display.

5) Charles Mingus (1922–1979) was a leading African American jazz double bassist, composer, and bandleader. The Youth Center that opened in 2008 was named in his memory.

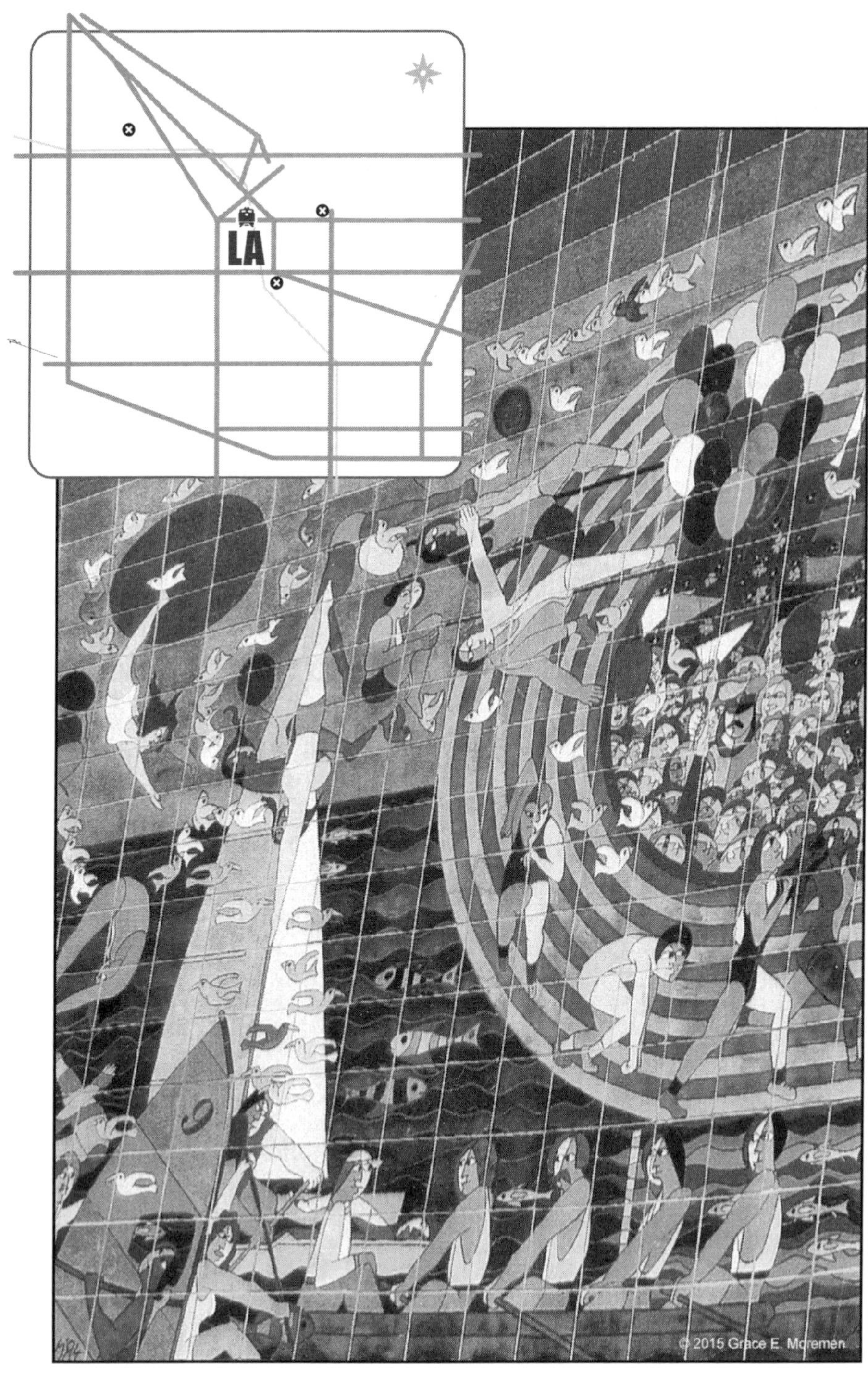
LA
© 2015 Grace E. Moremen

Murals Galore:

The Great Wall of Los Angeles and the Importance of Murals in LA

Tujunga Wash in Valley Glen
Boyle Heights • Cal State LA

These Adventures are very extensive and use several forms of transportation. ***You might want to see each one on a different day.*** *Murals can be found throughout Los Angeles, but we have chosen three areas to explore:*
(1) The Great Wall of LA in the San Fernando Valley
(2) Mural art in a residential neighborhood in East LA
(3) A hidden surprise at California State University, Los Angeles

To understand and appreciate the Los Angeles that has emerged since the riots of 1965 and 1992, it is helpful to look at some of the city's murals, the art of the people.[1]

The mural tradition goes back to 1932 when **David Alfaro Siqueiros** painted his powerful and controversial mural on a wall at **Olvera Street** (see Adventure 1). LA's year-round outdoor painting season, added to a city full of creative people, equals a very favorable climate for mural painting. As a result, murals have become LA's predominant art form and a powerful way to highlight the city's Mexican and indigenous roots.[2]

1) The idea to include murals in our Adventures came from David Oxtoby's *47 Things Every [Pomona] College Student Should See in Southern California Before Graduating.* We are also indebted to muralist and UCLA Professor of Art, Judith F. Baca, who spoke in a PBS interview of the importance of public art for people in the Latino community, many of whom rarely visit art museums. For over 30 years, her organization—the Social and Public Art Resource Center (SPARC)—has supported the creation of hundreds of murals across Los Angeles and elsewhere in the county.

2) Judith F. Baca, "The Art of the Mural." pbs.org/americanfamily/mural.html

MURALS • Part One

*In the San Fernando Valley, a spectacular mural can be found on the wall of the Tujunga Flood Control Channel, better known as the "**Tujunga Wash**."*

 *1½ miles max*  *4-5 hours*  *no fees*

Pack a picnic or buy a sandwich before starting out. Also, pick up a schedule for MTA **Local bus #154** at the east end of Union Station. Take the Metro **Red Line to the North Hollywood Station,** a ride of about forty minutes. Catch the **MTA Local #154 bus outside of the station at Bay 10.** It is a ten-minute ride to **Oxnard Street and Coldwater Canyon Road,** where you exit the bus.

*Note: **Restrooms** are located at Valley College on Oxnard Boulevard, just to the west of the mural.

The Manzanar section of *The Great Wall of Los Angeles*

The mural is located directly across the street from the bus stop. Extending for over half a mile, its size is astonishing, as it is one of the longest murals in the world.

15

The Great Wall of Los Angeles

12920 West Oxnard Street
Valley Glen, CA 91401

Conceived of and designed by **Judith F. Baca,** the mural was painted from the mid-1970s to the mid-1980s by over 400 artists, many of whom were high school students. Its vibrant colors tell the history of Los Angeles from prehistoric times to the 1984 Olympic Games. Not a typical textbook rendition, ***The Great Wall of Los Angeles*** depicts the accumulation of experiences and contributions of Native Americans, Latinos, African Americans, Asian Americans, as well as European Americans, in episodes of history often omitted from social studies courses. Some of the teenagers recruited by Ms. Baca to paint the mural were members of rival gangs. The common task of depicting their own story enabled them to work together peacefully, and participants have said that the experience was life-changing. Each artist's name is recorded on the wall. From 2009 to 2011, the mural was restored; the colors are now once again vivid and stunning. It has never been vandalized.

Start at the beginning and walk along the mural. The first pictures depict the **La Brea Tar Pits** in prehistoric times. Follow the centuries and decades to the mural's conclusion: the 1984 Summer Olympic Games in Los Angeles. In between, a story is revealed of human courage, suffering, greed, rebellion, endurance, and achievement, creatively woven together through the medium of painting.

An additional choice: If you would enjoy a 2.5 mile nature walk along the greenway of the Tujunga Wash, begin at Oxnard Street and walk south along the full length of the mural and continue walking until you reach Victory Boulevard. Make a U-turn and walk back on the west side of the wash. Cross Oxnard Street and continue walking north until you reach Burbank Boulevard. Make another U-turn and walk back on the east side of the wash to Oxnard Street, your starting point.

Look for the bus stop in front of the mural on the south side of Oxnard Street. **Catch the #154 Local bus and return to the North Hollywood Metro Station. Take the Red Line back to Union Station.**

A Metro Local bus crossing the First Street Bridge over the Los Angeles River

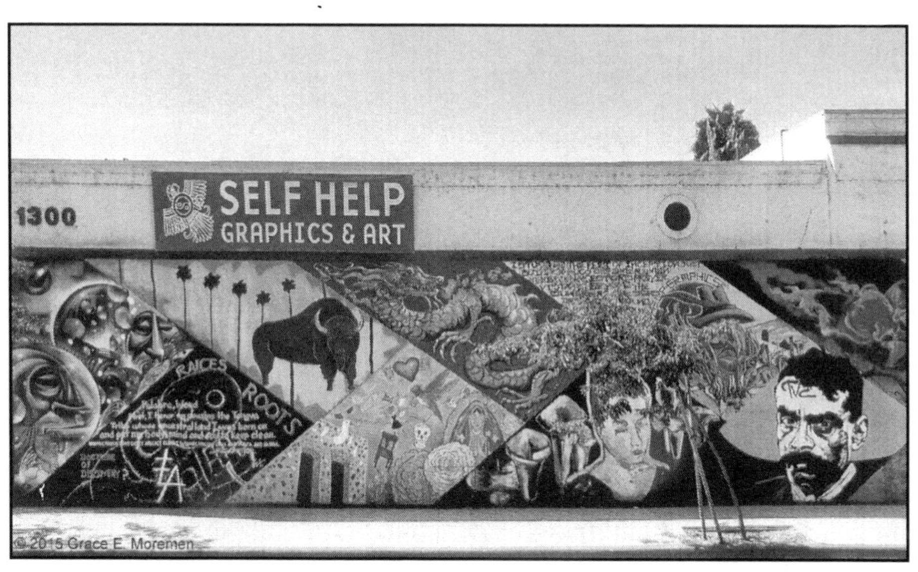

© 2015 Grace E. Moremen

MURALS • Part Two

*The **Boyle Heights** neighborhood of **East Los Angeles** is also a rich source of mural art and Mexican culture.*

 *1½ miles max*  *4–5 hours*  *no fees*

From Union Station, take the Gold Line, direction "East LA, Atlantic Boulevard." As you travel along East First Street, coming up very soon on your left at #815 is the beautiful **Nishi Hongwanji Buddhist Temple,** a reminder that you are still in Little Tokyo (Adventure 6). A bit farther along on, at 1300 East First Street on your right, notice the murals on the walls of **Self Help Graphics.**[3] Continue on the Gold Line and exit at the **Soto Street Station,** then **transfer to**

3) Self Help Graphics is a community-based program. Their building is pictured in a print on display at La Plaza de Cultura y Artes (Adventure 1).

the southbound #605 Local orange bus. Get off the bus at Olympic Boulevard in order to view the murals at Estrada Courts Apartments, located in a pleasant, tree-shaded neighborhood that extends from 3200 to 3300 East Olympic Boulevard. You will see the powerful mural, ***We Are Not a Minority,*** as well as many others as you walk along Olympic. It is possible to walk on the private property to view murals on the interior walls, but please be respectful of the residents. Catch the **northbound #605 Local bus (direction of USC Medical Center) and return to the Gold Line Soto Street Station.**

If you have enough time and the inclination, there is a remarkable Mexican marketplace (called ***El Mercadito***) nearby. Take the **eastbound Gold Line train, direction "East LA Atlantic Blvd." Exit at the next station, which is Indiana Street. Walk west on First Street (back toward downtown) for two blocks.** On your way you will pass the La Gloria tortilla factory. Notice the old grinding stones mounted on

A colorful mural at Estrada Courts by E. de la Loza, 1976

El Mercadito

Mexican Market Place
1st & Lorena, Boyle Heights
elmercadodelosangeles.com

the wall. **You will see that *El Mercadito* is ahead on your right. It's a three-level indoor shopping complex with two huge Mexican restaurants.** Turn right on the side street and enter through the parking lot at the rear. If you enjoyed Olvera Street, you will adore this place for buying gifts and cultural objects, or just to window shop. The colorful merchandise seems to go on forever. The two largest restaurants are located on the third floor, with smaller establishments at ground level. All serve delicious, fresh, authentic Mexican cuisine.

Get back on the Gold Line (direction of Sierra Madre). For another interesting detour, exit at the **Mariachi Plaza Station.** Enjoy the circular decorative patterns in the floor and the canopy of colored glass that sheds its colors of light on you as you come up the escalator. Prominent in the plaza is the statue of **Lucha Reyes** (1906–1944), a popular Mexican singer of mariachi music who broke the gender barrier for women in this field. Notice the large mural beside ***Santa Cecilia Comida Mexicana*** (where the food is reputed to be excellent). The mural is entitled ***El Corrido de Ricardo Valdez***, painted by **Juan Solis** in 1994. Mariachi Plaza is so named for the musicians who wait here on weekends to be hired for special occasions. Across the street is the recently restored nineteenth-century **Boyle Heights Hotel** (now an office building). This area of the city, lively with mural art on almost every corner, has a flavor all its own. **Reboard the Gold Line** for your ride back to **Union Station.**

MURALS • Part Three

*The campus of **California State University, Los Angeles** is located about three miles **east of Union Station** on the **Metrolink San Bernardino Line.** Cal State LA was founded in 1947. Groundbreaking for the first buildings on its present campus took place in 1955. One of its most famous graduates is tennis great **Billie Jean King.***

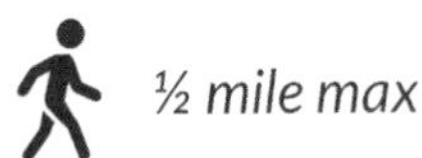
½ mile max

3 hours

no fees

From Union Station, take the Metrolink San Bernardino Line and exit at Cal State LA. Ride the elevator up one level, and then take another elevator to the very top. Walk a short distance to your left and then turn right onto the main thoroughfare into the campus. Your destination is the **gymnasium,** which is about a quarter of a mile up the road on your right. There is a large campus map on a bulletin board on your left to help you find the gym.

On the outside wall of the gym you will see a large tile mural, entitled ***Olympic Fantasy,*** created by **Guillermo Wagner Granizo** (1923–1995) for the 1984 Summer Olympic Games held in Los Angeles. A large oval track is its centerpiece and the panorama shows athletes competing in many different sports. Cal State LA was the venue for Olympic competition in judo wrestling, which took place in this gymnasium. The mural was restored in 2012 and its colors are bright and vibrant.[4]

After viewing this mural, go into the gym. In the lobby, look for a door with a glass window on your right. It opens onto a corridor that

4) Murals were commissioned to be installed all over Los Angeles to celebrate the 1984 Summer Olympics. Many were painted along freeways. Not only did they celebrate the athletes, they celebrated the city as well.

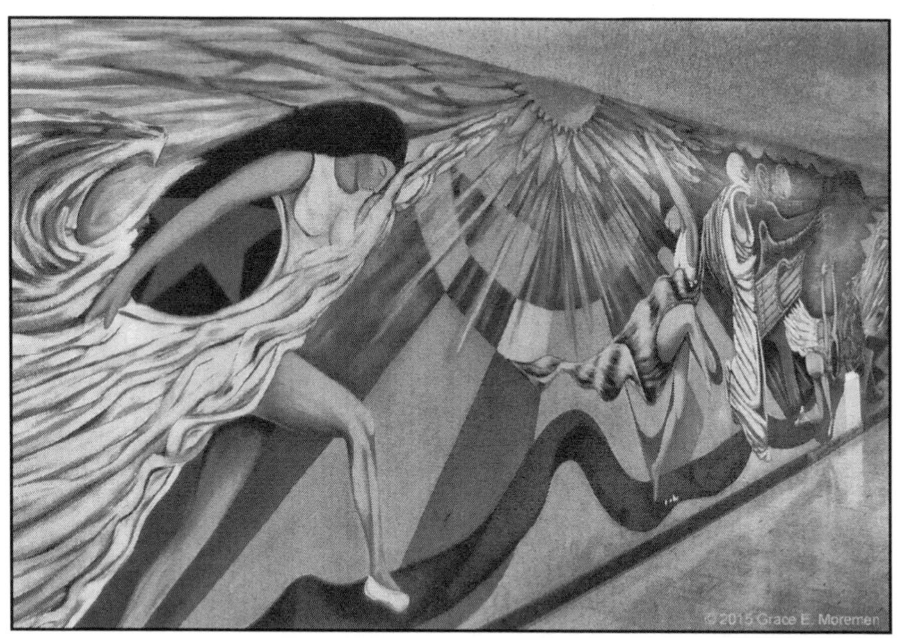

Cal State LA

5151 State University Dr.

323-343-3000 • calstatela.edu

leads to the dance department. Now comes your surprise. Open the door and be prepared to be amazed at what you see: a mural that completely covers both walls of the corridor from floor to ceiling with life-sized dancing figures. Look for the self-portrait of the artist **Ismael Cazarez** in the corner near the door, and the angel reaching down to touch him.[5] Because it has been protected inside the building, the mural's colors are still strong. Painted in 1979, it is a unique creation and well worth taking time to see it.

You might want to linger longer on the campus. There is a cafeteria a little farther up the road. **Then retrace your steps back to the elevator and the Metro station.**

5) A native Angeleno of Mexican heritage, Ismael Cazarez earned a master's degree from Cal State Los Angeles. His murals can be found throughout the Los Angeles area.

LA

Echo Park

Only minutes away by bus from downtown LA, Echo Park is both a lovely park and one of the oldest districts in the city. The park is bordered by Echo Park Avenue on the east and Glendale Boulevard on the west, with a small lake, created in the 1860s to serve as a reservoir, nestled in the middle. Today it serves as a water collection basin for the city's storm drain system.

 *1 mile max*  *2–3 hours*  *no fees*

To get there from Union Station, take the Red or Purple Line to Civic Center. Walk north on Hill Street one block to Temple Street. Then catch the **MTA #92 Local orange bus** at the stop on the **northeast corner of Temple and Hill.** There are three bus stops at the park.

From 2011 to 2013, the park went through a major reconstruction and restoration. The lake was completely drained and a new lake bed and retaining walls were built. Reopened in June 2013, **Echo Park Lake** now offers a clean, safe, and welcoming place for a stroll, a paddle boat ride, a picnic, or family celebrations.[1] Here you can sit and enjoy the sight of three giant waterspouts, water lilies, and many kinds of birds. In June, Echo Park hosts the **Lotus Festival.**

1) On one of her visits, Grace enjoyed seeing a wedding party taking pictures beside the lake.

Echo Park

751 Echo Park Avenue

As you look toward the south end of the lake, you have a nice view of the skyline of downtown Los Angeles in the distance. And don't forget to take a look at the sculpture that stands beside the lake, ***Our Lady of the Angels,*** known locally as "The Lady of the Lake." It was created by sculptor **Ada May Sharpness** (1899–1988) and erected here by the Federal Art Project (1934–1935), recently restored by the City of Los Angeles Cultural Affairs Department.[2]

A café is located on the east side of the lake, and **Restrooms** are nearby. Placed at intervals around the lakeshore are a number of observation platforms with information about its importance as a wetlands habitat. There is an attractive **children's playground** at the north end of the lake, and **paddle boats** can be rented at the boathouse.

2) Information from a plaque on the base of the sculpture.

Echo Park hosts the Lotus Festival every June.

You may notice an impressive-looking building north of the park. This is the **Angelus Temple,** dedicated in 1923 and once the home of the International Foursquare Gospel Church founded by evangelist **Aimee Semple McPherson** (1890–1944). Now designated a National Historic Landmark, it is home to the **Hispanic Church of Angelus Temple.** On the east side of the lake you will see the headquarters of the **Los Angeles Diocese of the Episcopal Church,** which moved to this site in 1994.

A little-known fact is that the earliest movies made in Los Angeles were filmed in this district, originally called "Edendale." The **Selig-Polyscope Studios** moved here from Chicago in 1909, specializing in "westerns" with cowboy actor **Tom Mix** (1880–1940). The **Mack Sennett Studios** followed in 1912, becoming best known for the Keystone Comedies featuring the popular **Keystone Cops.**[3] You can still see Sennett's sound stage building located a few blocks north of the park

3) Mack Sennett (1880–1960) was born in Canada.

© 2015 Grace E. Moremen

© 2015 Grace E. Moremen

at 1712 Glendale Boulevard (now repurposed as a public storage facility). In 1982, this building was granted National Historic Landmark status.

When you leave Echo Park, we suggest returning by another route. Walk one block north on **Echo Park Avenue to Sunset Boulevard.** The bus stop is on the southwest corner of Echo Park Avenue and Sunset. Catch the **#704 Rapid Red bus** back to Union Station.

For a meal we suggest **Taix French Restaurant.** Top-rated and family friendly, it was established in 1927 ($9–$30). **Located at 1911 Sunset Boulevard** on the north side of the boulevard, it is near the corner of Sunset and Park Avenue. **Reservations suggested: 213-484-1265.**

To get to Taix from the park, walk to the north end of the park. Cross Glendale Boulevard and take Park Avenue, which angles to the left. Walk one block on Park to Sunset Boulevard. Taix is right across the street.

When you are ready to catch the bus back to Union Station, **walk three blocks east on Sunset to Echo Park Avenue, cross to the southwest corner, and look for the stop for the #704 Rapid red bus.** Remember, it is free with your Metrolink ticket.

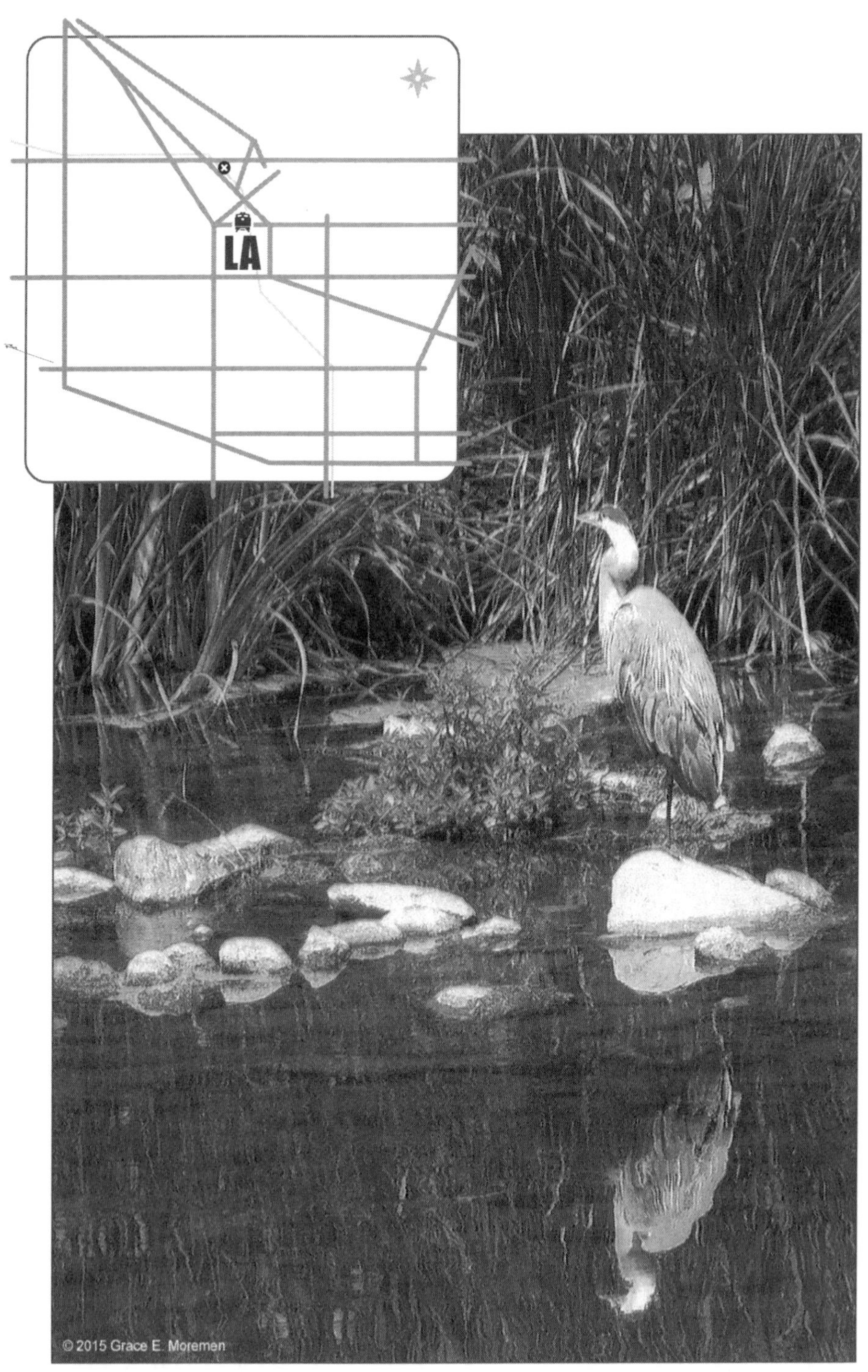
LA
© 2015 Grace E. Moremen

17

"Down by the Riverside"

The Los Angeles River Greenway

*Why would you want to spend several hours of your valuable free time going to visit a river that is little more than a storm drain? That's a legitimate question. What you may not know is that the word "drain" describes only one characteristic of the Los Angeles River. There is another side to its character, a green side, with many delightful attributes to be admired and enjoyed. It is the purpose of this Adventure to help you discover that other side: the amiable and refreshing LA River Greenway.**

 *1 mile max*  *2-3 hours*  *no fees*

It is a fact that without the river, there would be no Los Angeles. It was the life-giving water source for the fledgling *pueblo* at its founding in 1781 and for the city as it grew until an aqueduct was built in 1913, bringing water from the north. Over the years, the river has regularly flooded when winter rains were especially heavy. However, in times past, before so much ground was paved over in Los Angeles, the flood waters had room to spread out and could be absorbed. For complex reasons, by the winter of 1938, the city was ripe for a disastrous flood. Two Pacific storms that year in February and March brought an

* Much of the background information for Adventure 17 is from the beautiful book, *Rio LA: Tales from the Los Angeles River*, by Patt Morrison, as cited in the Introduction.

The Los Angeles River Greenway

Atwater District

larivercorp.com/greenway2020

abnormally high amount of rainfall that transformed the docile stream into a raging torrent that destroyed everything in its path and caused 115 deaths. As a result, the Army Corps of Engineers was called in to encase the river in cement, to make it a "flood control" channel, and the fact that it was a green and living river was conveniently forgotten or ignored.

However, because of underground springs, it was impossible to cement the river bottom in three sections: the **Tujunga Wash** in the San Fernando Valley, the **Del Amo** section north of Long Beach, and the section near **Atwater Village** across from **Griffith Park.** In all these sections, plants grew up, but were always cut back. In Atwater, over the years, the area was not maintained, trash accumulated, and this part of the river became an eyesore.

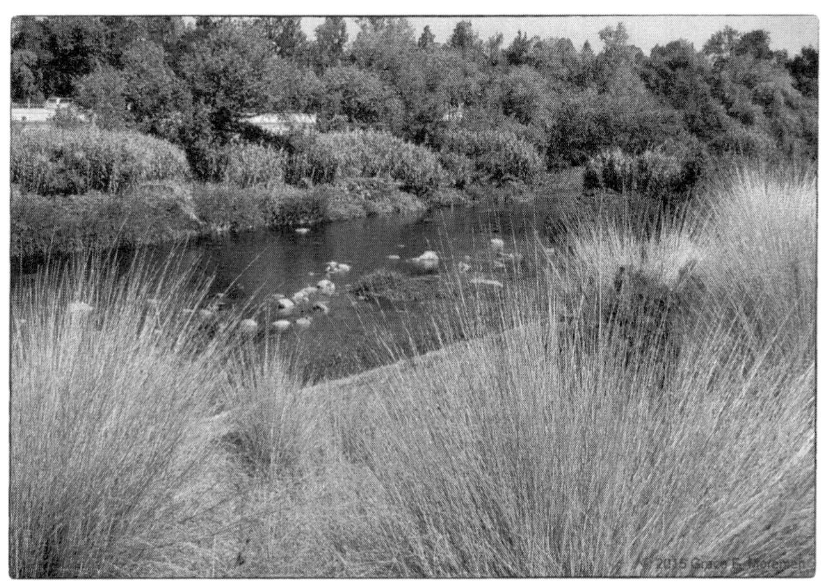

Soft grasses beside the river at Atwater, looking north

Glendale Narrows, looking south

In the 1990s, a group of citizens persuaded the city government that if plantings were cared for (instead of mowed down) and riverside pathways built, a greenway could be created that all Angelenos could enjoy. And so it has happened. Today, this part of the riverbank is lush with trees, shrubs, and marsh grasses, and provides habitat for birds, fish, and other creatures. There are even sections where kayaking takes place. Yet, in **Atwater,** because the shoreline is hidden by trees, fences, and other impediments, **travelers on nearby streets or whizzing by on Interstate 5 cannot see that the beautiful Los Angeles River Greenway lies just a short distance away.** To help you reach the Atwater section by public transportation is the purpose of Adventure 17.[1]

Bring a picnic or buy a sandwich before you start out. Pick up a schedule for MTA Local bus #180 at the east end of Union Station.

Take the **Metro Red Line and get off at the Sunset/Vermont**

[1] There is an **LA River Center and Gardens** that is located in a lovely facility at 570 West 26th Street, Los Angeles, in the **Cypress Park** district. Open Monday through Friday from 9:00am to 5:00pm, it often features excellent exhibits. The office of the **Friends of the LA River** is also headquartered there. Unfortunately, the riverside greenway is not accessible from the center. **www.folar.org**

Station in Hollywood. As you emerge from the station, you will be facing Vermont Avenue. Take a right on Vermont and walk two blocks (toward the mountains) to Prospect Avenue. Cross at the light and continue on Vermont a short way until you see the bus stop for the **MTA #180 Local orange bus.** The bus will be marked **"Altadena-Pasadena."** It is a fifteen-minute ride to the river.

After you cross the river on the **Los Feliz Bridge,**[2] get off at the first stop, **Glen Feliz Avenue.** Cross **Los Feliz Boulevard** at the light. There is a café handy where you can get a cup of coffee and/or use the **Restroom.**

To reach the greenway, walk back toward the river on the sidewalk on Los Feliz Boulevard. Just before the bridge, you will see a decorative archway on your right that leads to the riverside path. Go through the archway, turn right, and walk along the path. You are on the east side of

[2] This bridge is one of eleven scenic and historic bridges that span the Los Angeles River. They were built during the first third of the twentieth century as part of a nationwide "City Beautiful" movement. From north to south the bridges are: (1) Los Feliz, 1925, (2) Hyperion/Glendale, 1929, (3) North Broadway, 1909, (4) North Spring, 1928, (5) North Main, 1910, (6) Macy Street/Cesar Chavez Ave., 1926, (7) East First Street, 1939, (8) East Fourth Street, 1930, (9) East Sixth Street, 1932, (10) East Seventh Street, 1927, and (11) East Ninth Street, 1925.

The River Center, which is a couple of miles south of the Atwater section

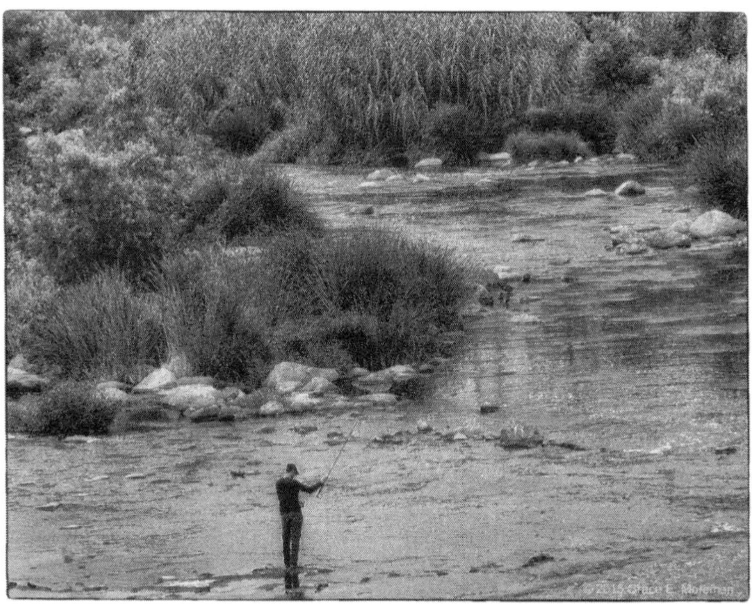

Fisherman south of Hyperion Bridge

the river. You may be treated to the sight of a great blue heron standing on the opposite bank, or you might spot mallard ducks, wild geese, and many smaller birds.[3] The flowing water and the natural environment can have a soothing effect.

Continue your walk (north) for about a mile to your next destination, **North Atwater Park**, an attractive "pocket park" with picnic tables and an informational display about the river. **Restrooms** are located in the second parking lot.

For your return trip, walk back to Los Feliz Boulevard and turn left. The **#180 Local bus stop** will be a little way up, on the same side of the street. **The bus will be marked "Hollywood & Vine."**

Get off the bus at **Hollywood and Western. Cross Hollywood Boulevard, and the Metro Station** is right in front of you. **Catch the Red Line back to Union Station.**

---

[3] Grace saw a great blue heron standing on an open lawn while she was riding on the miniature train in Griffith Park. She wondered, "Why here?" till she realized that the Atwater greenway section of the river is only a short flight over the treetops from Griffith Park.

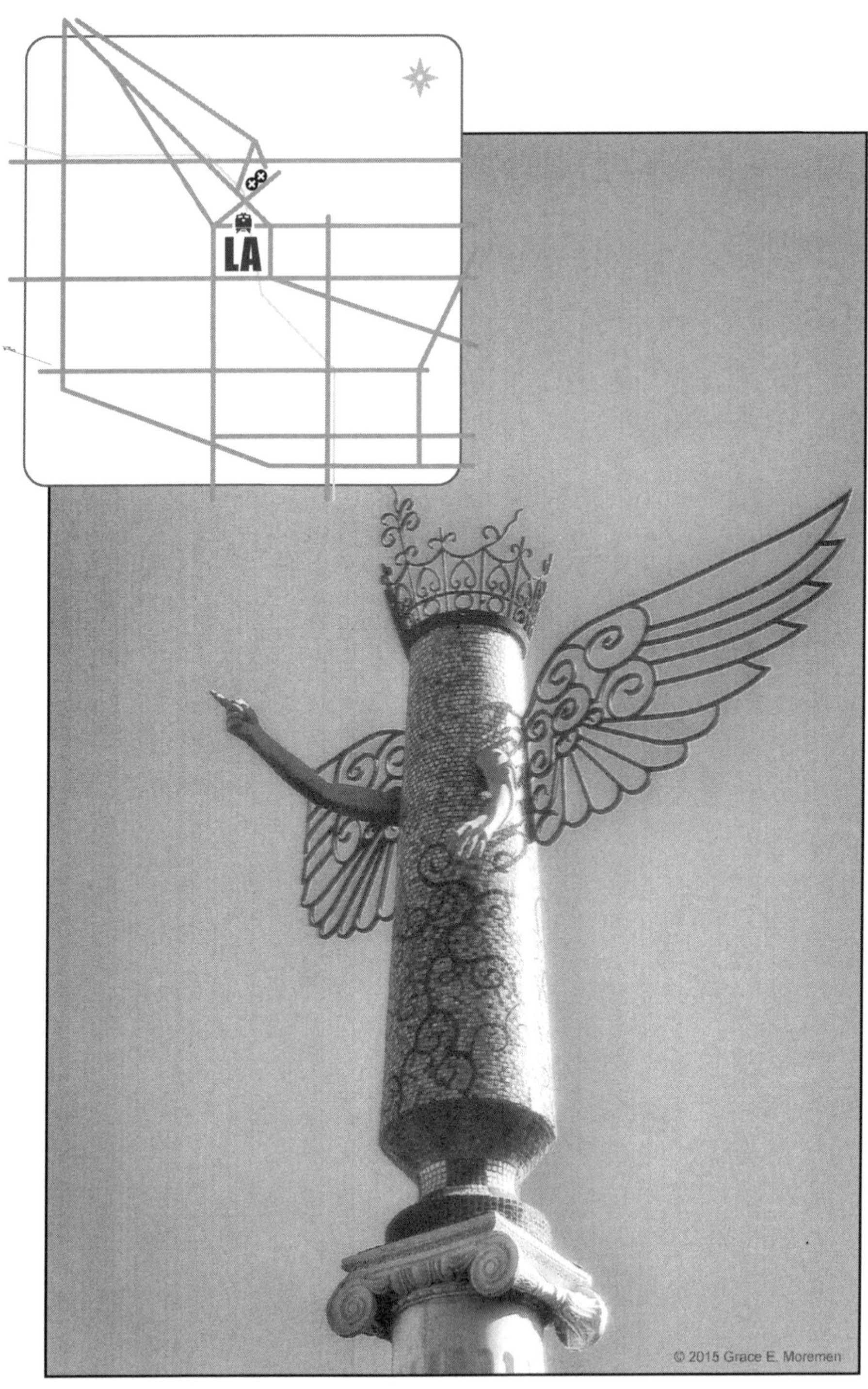
LA
© 2015 Grace E. Moremen

18

Two Stars in Highland Park:

The Southwest Museum, The Lummis House, and a Walk Through the Neighborhood

This Adventure in northeast Los Angeles takes you into the historic district of Highland Park to visit two of its cultural stars: the Southwest Museum, the oldest museum in Los Angeles, and Lummis House, home of the museum's principal founder. It also includes a walk through the attractive neighborhood of North Figueroa Street, where some engaging surprises await the visitor. This old and settled neighborhood with its tranquil, venerable museum is the kind of place that seems to beckon one to return, time and time again.

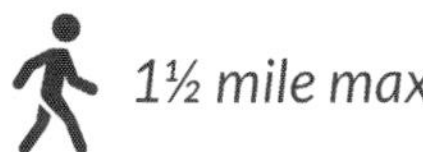

From Union Station, take the Gold Line north (direction "Sierra Madre") four stops to the Southwest Museum Station. As you disembark, see if you can find the four whimsical figures atop tall columns around the station platform. The figures are made of tile with lacy wings of aluminum. They are known as the **Guardians** of the residents of **Highland Park** and the riders of the **Gold Line.** Their creator, Highland Park resident artist **Teddy Sandoval,** continues his whimsical theme in the design of the seats in the station and other ornate objects.[1]

1) lacitypix.wordpress.com/tag/art-at-southwest-museum/

Southwest Museum: Mt. Washington Campus

234 Museum Drive

323-221-2163 • southwestmuseum.org/mt-washington

Open Saturdays only • 10:00am–4:00pm • Free

As you leave the station, look up to see your first destination nestled on the slopes of Mount Washington. **The Southwest Museum of the American Indian** is LA's oldest museum. Opened at this site in 1913, it is on the U.S. Register of Historic Places and is also a Los Angeles Historic–Cultural Monument. The architects were **Sumner P. Hunt** and **Silas R. Burns,** who both collaborated with the museum's principal founder, **Charles Fletcher Lummis** (1859–1928). Lummis wanted the building to reflect the Spanish heritage of Los Angeles, and so the museum's signature tower was modeled after the tower of the Alhambra Palace in Spain.

Roadrunner design, Zia Pueblo, twentieth century

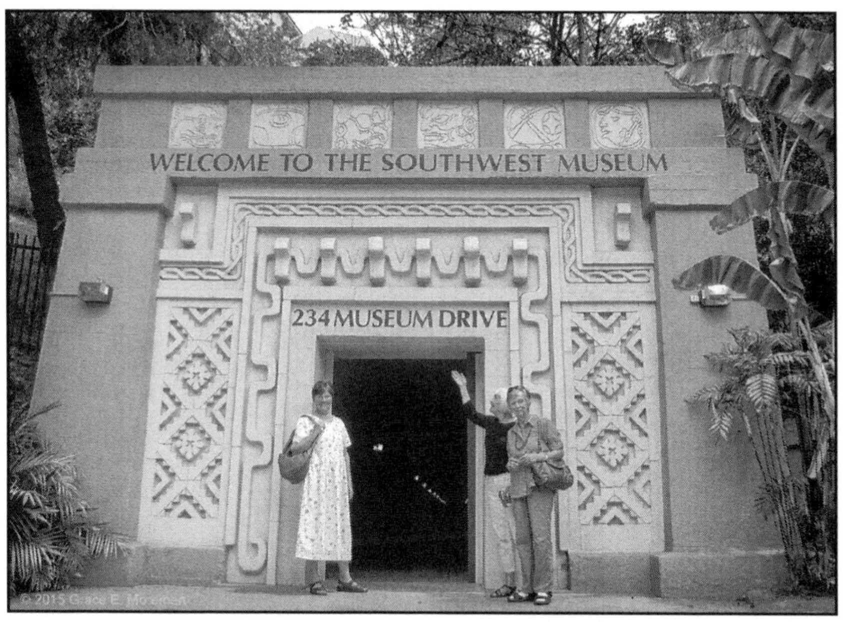

Janet, Jacqueline, and Lynne invite you into the museum's impressive entrance.

Cross over the Gold Line tracks, cross the street, and walk half a block on Museum Drive to the main entrance. This striking doorway is in the *Mayan Revival* style.[2] Inside, walk along the 240-foot corridor that leads to the elevator that will transport you to the building above. Go to the second floor, and walk up a short flight of stairs to the main exhibition hall.

The hall is quiet and inviting with its high ceiling and excellent lighting. On the day we were there, the rotating exhibit showed the museum's stunning collection of southwest pottery spanning four centuries. All of the pieces were well displayed and documented, and the atmosphere was meditative and reflective. The docents were friendly, helpful, and knowledgeable.

The museum's world-famous collection contains over 250,000 artifacts that range from the prehistoric to the present period. It is under the aegis of the **Autry National Center's Southwest Museum**

2) *Los Angeles: An Architectural Guide* by Gebhard and Winter.

Preservation Project, which does the work of inventory, preservation, conservation, and installation of the artifacts.

Restrooms are available. If you have brought a picnic, you will find tables and chairs in the patio.

Adjacent to the patio is the **Braun Research Library,** established in 1977. It contains extensive materials on the cultures of the Native American peoples and on the history of the American West. **Reservations are required. Call 323-221-2164, extension 256.**

Take the elevator to return to the street, or walk down the **Hopi Trail** through the museum's **Ethnobotanical Garden.** The trail is steep but there are handrails along the descent.

To reach the **Lummis House,** return to the **Gold Line Station and walk across both sets of tracks and down the steps to Figueroa Street below. Turn right and walk to Avenue 43. Go left to 200 East Avenue 43.** The entrance to the house is around the corner.

Lummis House is also known as ***El Alisal,*** named for the large sycamore tree in the patio. Charles Lummis built the house, largely with his own hands, over a period of fourteen years between 1896 and 1910, using stones from the nearby arroyo and railroad supports for the ceiling beams. The architecture is considered to have been the catalyst for the birth of the **Arts and Crafts movement** in Southern California.[3] Lummis's main salon, or the *Museo,* is spacious and comfortable with hand-hewn wooden furniture and cabinets. Most impressive are the photographs and glass negatives embedded in the windows. In the open guest book one can see the signatures of many famous people of the day who were entertained here, such as **John Muir** and **Carl Sandberg.**

---

3) The crowning gems of the Arts and Crafts architectural movement were homes such as the famous Gamble House (1908–1909), designed by the brothers Charles Sumner Greene (1868–1957) and Henry Mather Greene (1870–1954), known as Greene & Greene.
www.mota.dreamhosters.com/lummis-home-and-garden

Lummis House

200 E. Avenue 43

323-222-0546

Hours: Friday–Sunday 12noon – 4pm

Admission free

Standing in this house, one feels the vibrancy and vitality of both the man and his guests. Lummis, a Massachusetts native and graduate of Harvard University, had fallen in love with the Southwest and its people[4] when he walked from Ohio to Southern California in 1884 (taking 143 days) to take a job with the brand-new *Los Angeles Times* as its first city editor. Besides being a journalist, Lummis was an author, anthropologist, and photographer. It was in 1907 that he and the Southwest Society founded the Southwest Museum.[5]

4) Reportedly, the people of the Southwest also loved Charles Lummis; their descendants continue to visit Lummis House to honor him and his friendship. (www.tripadvisor.com)
5) www.mota.dreamhosters.com/lummis-home-and-garden

Return to Figueroa Street and turn right. Walk north to 4671 to see the **Glenmary Archway** that dates from 1903. Muralists **Paola Lopez, Heriberto Luna,** and a team of fifteen young artists covered the archway with a wonderfully colorful mural in 2010. It is titled ***Haramokngа*, meaning "the place where people gather."** This location had once been a stop on the **Pacific Electric Trolley** line, and many years before a gathering place for indigenous people.[6] Across the street is the beautiful fifteen-acre **Sycamore Grove Park** at 4702 North Figueroa on the banks of the **Arroyo Seco.** In the park is the Sousa-Hiner Band Shell built by bandmaster Dr. Edwin C. Hiner in honor of his dear friend, John Philip Sousa.

Continue up Figueroa Street to Avenue 50. Go left across the street to Sycamore Terrace to see **five *Craftsman*-style bungalows** called **"Faculty Row."** They were built prior to 1914 for professors at nearby **Occidental College** before it relocated to Eagle Rock.[7]

6) *[View] from a Loft* (blog) www.viewfromaloft.org, November 21, 2010.
7) *KCET*: www.kcet.org/social/departures/fieldguides/highlandpark/walking-sightseeing/southwest-museum-gold-line-station.html

Walk north from Avenue 50 to Avenue 60 to enjoy a newly revitalized neighborhood. In the summer of 2014 the **mayor of Los Angeles, Eric Garcetti,** identified this area as part of his **"Great Streets" program.** Garcetti's vision is to create new, exciting neighborhoods in a dozen or more areas that show potential for increased pedestrian activity. The plan is to add bike racks, new plazas, upgraded crosswalks, and other such enhancements in hope that people will stay in their own neighborhoods to shop, eat at local cafes, and enjoy new public spaces near their homes.[8]

Return to the Gold Line Station, either by walking back on **Figueroa Street** or by catching the **MTA Local #81 orange bus.** Take the **southbound train marked "East LA"** and exit at **Union Station.**

Descending the Hopi Trail, Southwest Museum

8) From "Urban Acupuncture" by David Zahniser, Matt Stevens, and Laura J. Nelson, *Los Angeles Times,* July 27, 2014, front page.

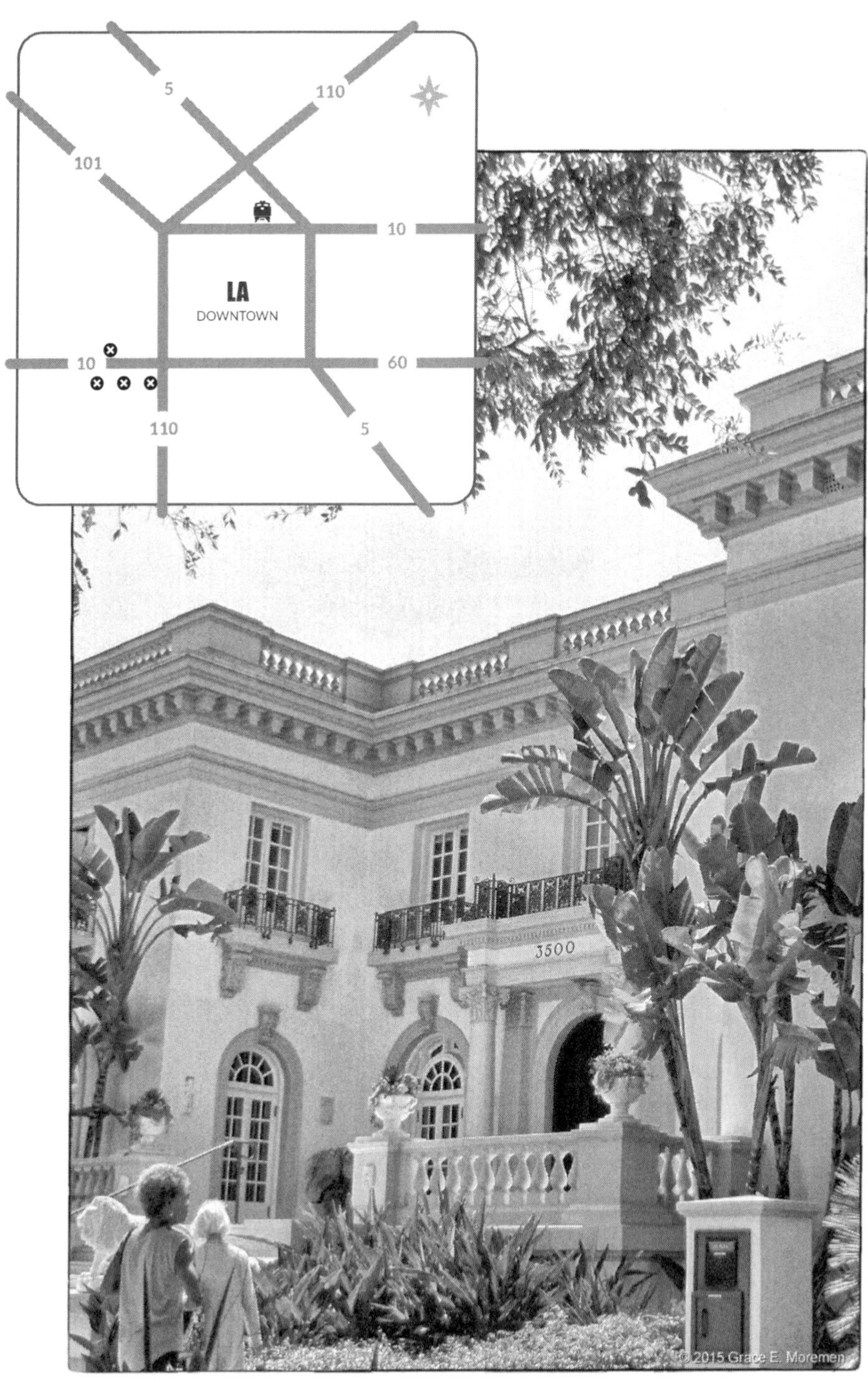
5
110
101
10
LA
DOWNTOWN
10
60
110
5
3500
© 2015 Grace E. Moremen

The Beauties of West Adams

Lots & Lots of Cool Houses Peace Awareness Labyrinth & Gardens • The Congregational Church of Christian Fellowship (United Church of Christ)

As Los Angeles grew at the turn of the twentieth century, the corridor along West Adams Boulevard, south of downtown, became the location of choice for wealthy Angelenos to build their homes. During a thirty-five-year period, from about 1890 to the mid-1920s, an incredible number of mansions sprouted up, all within a few miles of each other. Although many have been torn down over the years, a significant number have remained—some palatial, some quirky, but all beautiful and unique in their own way. They are an important part of LA's history and the sight of them is not to be missed. The neighborhood has a long tradition of African American culture, and recently has grown increasingly Latino.

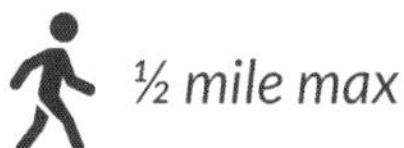

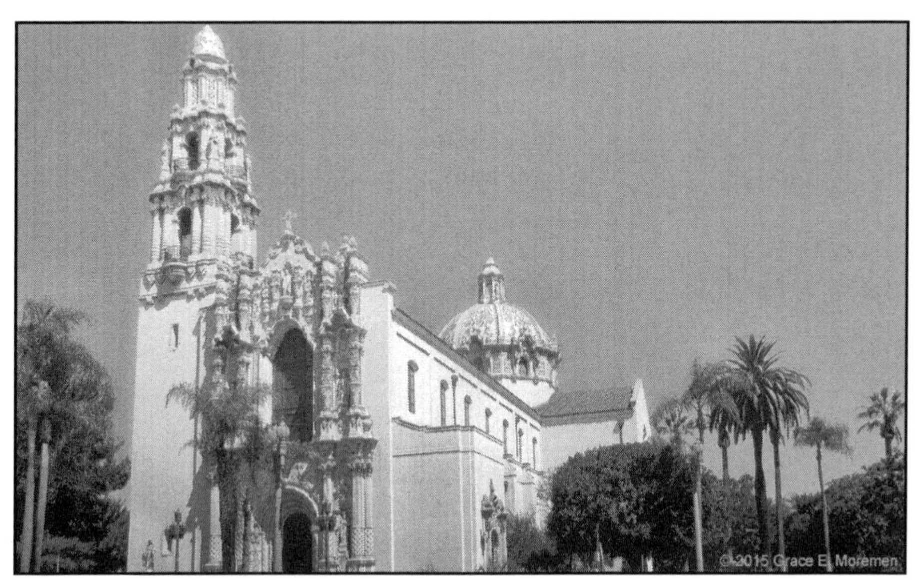

St. Vincent de Paul Catholic Church
(1920s Mission Revival)

St. John's Episcopal Cathedral
(Romanesque Revival)

Before leaving Union Station, pick up a schedule for the **#37 Local bus,** and **also the #207 Local.** Take the **Red or Purple line** to **Pershing Square Station.** Exit the station and **walk west on Fifth Street for three blocks to Grand Avenue.** The stop for the **westbound #37** is on the **west side of Grand Avenue** in the middle of the block.

Get off the bus at **West Adams Boulevard and Figueroa Street.** You may be struck by the sight of three imposing and impressive buildings built in the 1920s: **St. Vincent de Paul Catholic Church** on the corner opposite with its tile-covered dome; the **Automobile Club of Southern California,** an imposing building located on the other corner (both *Mission Revival* style); and **St. John's Episcopal Cathedral** (*Romanesque Revival* style) located on the south side of West Adams. All three buildings have historic landmark status.

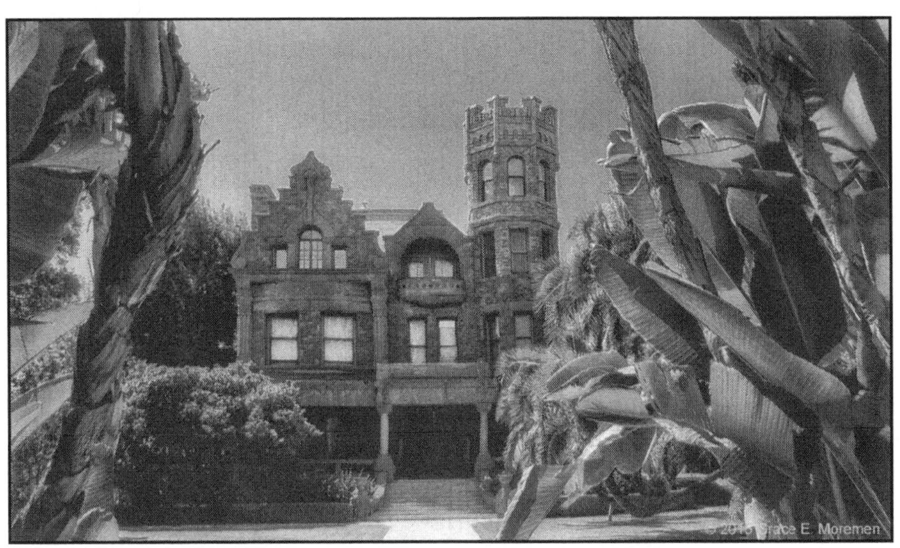

Stimson House
(1894)

For the sight of your first West Adams District mansion, cross Figueroa and turn right. Walk one block on Figueroa to the **Stimson House** (1894). This red sandstone "castle" is one of the oldest grand houses to have survived in West Adams. A kiosk in front tells the story of this building, which is now owned by an order of nuns.

Walk back to West Adams Boulevard, return to the bus stop, and **catch the next #37 to continue your journey westward along the boulevard.**

Doheny House
(1898-1900)

Almost immediately, you will pass by the **Doheny Campus** of **Mount Saint Mary's College,** just off West Adams to your right on the north side. Their property, situated on Chester Place and Saint James Place, includes the famous **Doheny House** (1898–1900). For information about visiting the campus and the Doheny House,
call 213-477-2500.

Other homes on West Adams of interest are listed below, in a westward progression:

948 West Adams: Second Church of Christ Scientist
(1905–1910 Beaux Arts style)

950 West Adams: Casa de Rosas
(1894 Mission Revival style)

1140 West Adams
(1892 Queen Anne style)

1325 West Adams: Kerckhoff House
(1900 Queen Anne/Colonial Revival style)

Continue your bus ride for approximately three miles. Your destination is the **Peace Awarenesss Labyrinth and Gardens. Go to their website ahead of time to make arrangements for your visit** and **get reservations for the buffet lunch.** Exit the bus at **Fourth Street. Cross Adams, turn right, and walk to 3500.** You may be surprised to see that

A grand house on Saint James Place, north of Adams

19

Peace Awareness Labyrinth & Gardens

3500 West Adams

peacelabyrinth.org

Hours: 12:00noon–4:00pm • Buffet lunch at 1:00pm • $8

you have arrived at a beautiful villa, built in 1910 during the heyday of West Adams.[1] There is an intercom unit at the front gate. Press the call button and say that you are here to see the Peace Awareness Labyrinth and the Meditation Garden, and that you have **reservations for lunch and for tour groups of five or more people.**[2]

This venue provides a quiet, renewing atmosphere that lifts the spirit. The carefully maintained grounds offer a remarkably tranquil space, set apart from the noisy world outside. **You are free to walk the labyrinth.** It is a flat stone surface, approximately forty feet across, patterned after

1) The mansion (in the *Italian Renaissance* style) was commissioned by the Guasti family in 1910. The family once owned a large vineyard and winery east of Ontario, California. Guided tours of the historic rooms of the mansion are available.

2) The house and grounds are owned and maintained by the Movement of Spiritual Inner Awareness.

Jacqueline ponders the journey ahead.

the labyrinth at Chartres Cathedral in France. An ancient form of spiritual practice, the labyrinth offers opportunity to experience peace and tranquility as one walks the single path that eventually leads to the center and then back out again.

Beyond the labyrinth, at a lower level on the grounds, is the Asian-inspired **Meditation Garden.** Beautifully laid out and landscaped, the garden contains many unique fountains, with a **peace obelisk** at its center. The atmosphere of both labyrinth and garden is deeply reverent.

For your return journey, catch **the #37 Local eastbound. Get off at Grand and Fifth and walk east on Fifth to the Pershing Square Station. Catch the Metro back to Union Station.**

An additional choice: a beautiful church

The stained-glass windows in this church that commemorate the **six historically African American Colleges in the United States** are well worth seeing. The church's beautiful architecture is a blend of *Mission Revival, Churrigueresque,* and *Spanish Gothic* styles. It was erected in 1941 by its first occupants, the Armenian Gesthemane Church, and later purchased by the **Congregational Church of Christian Fellowship** in 1963. It is primarily an African American congregation.[3]

To reach the church, take the **#37 Local bus** to **Adams and Western Avenue. Transfer to the #207 Local bus, northbound on Western. Get off at Washington Boulevard and walk one block east to Oxford Street. Turn right on Oxford and walk south. The church is on the corner of Oxford and South Hobart Boulevard.**[4]

3) The renowned Albert McNeil Jubilee Singers originated in this church, and the congregation has a long history of support for the Farm Workers' Movement and civil rights.

4) You will notice that the church is located right at the edge of the 10 Freeway. In the 1960s, construction for this freeway plowed right through "Sugar Hill" in the West Adams District, dividing neighborhoods and destroying many beautiful old homes.

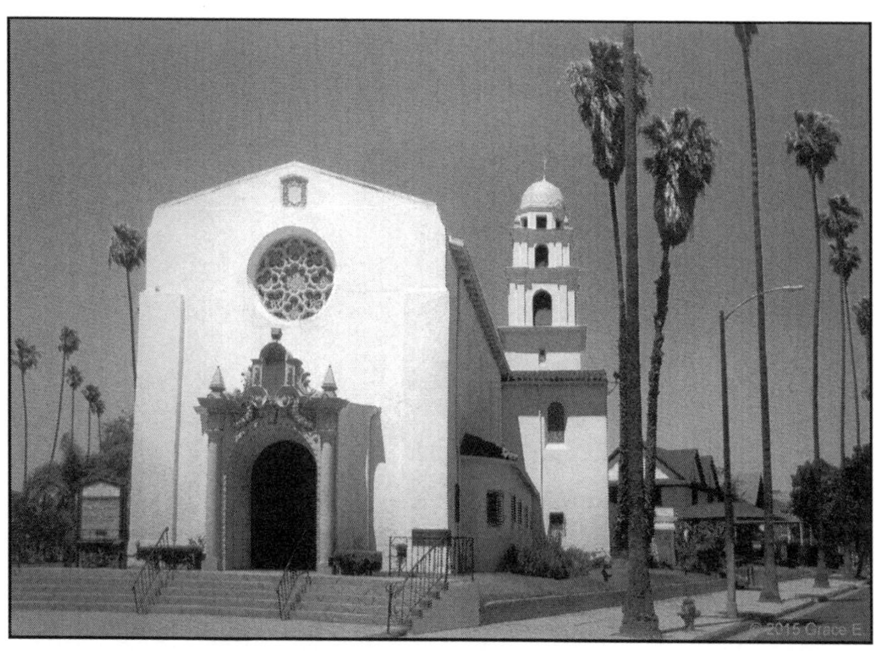

The Congregational Church of Christian Fellowship (United Church of Christ)

2085 South Hobart Boulevard

The church office is open Monday, Wednesday, & Friday

(Call 323-731-8869 to make arrangements)

To return to downtown LA, walk back to **Western Avenue.** Take the **#207 Local south** to **Adams Boulevard.** Transfer to the **#37 eastbound** on **Adams.** Exit at **Fifth and Grand,** turn right on **Fifth,** and proceed to the **Pershing Square Metro Station.** Catch the train back to **Union Station.**

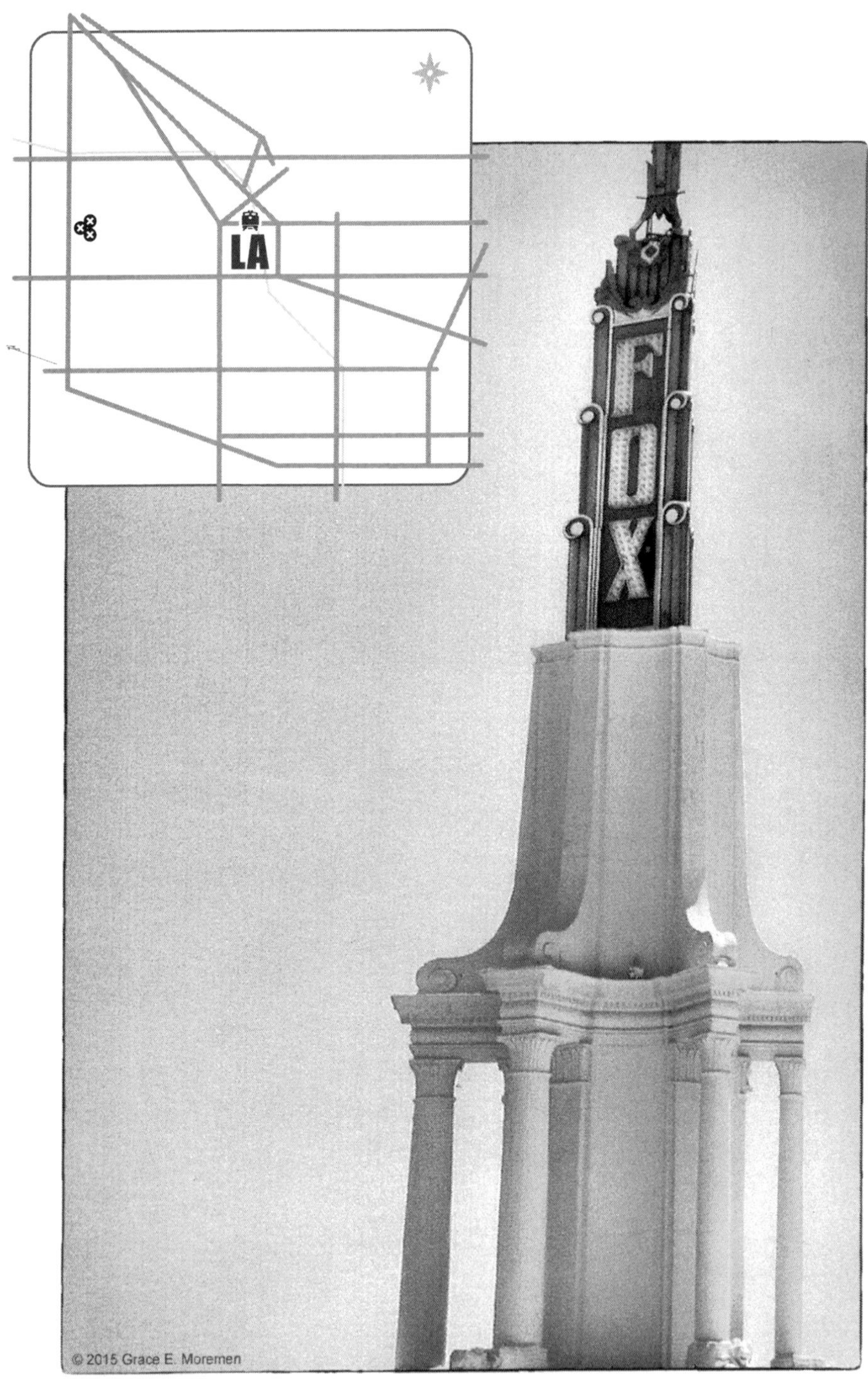
LA
FOX
© 2015 Grace E. Moremen

Westwood and UCLA

Hammer Museum • Fowler Museum
The Black Experience (mural)

Ten miles west of downtown LA, the community of Westwood wraps around the University of California, Los Angeles (UCLA). Adjacent to the campus, ***Westwood Village,*** *one of the earliest planned shopping centers in the country, still reflects the Spanish Colonial Revival architecture that prevailed at the time UCLA moved there in 1929. Since then, the once-fledgling university has experienced tremendous growth, becoming one of the premier research institutions in the world, with a large enrollment of over 42,000. Located on 419 acres of hilly land, the campus is beautiful, but its enormous size can be daunting to the visitor. To make your visit more doable,* ***Adventure 20 will focus on just three venues.***

 *2 miles max*  *5 hours* 

no fees!

From Union Station, take the Metro Purple Line to Wilshire and Western. Transfer to the #720 Rapid bus. Exit at Westwood Boulevard. Duration: approximately one hour from Union Station.

Located on the north side of Wilshire between Westwood Boulevard and Glendon Avenue, the **Hammer Museum of Art and Culture** offers an exciting and stimulating look at contemporary art. Named

Hammer Museum

10899 Wilshire Boulevard

310-443-7000 • www.hammer.ucla.edu

Tuesday–Friday • 11:00am–8:00pm

Saturday–Sunday • 11:00am–5:00pm

Closed Monday

Also closed July 4, Thanksgiving, Christmas, and New Year's Day

Admission is Free (charge for special exhibitions)

for its major benefactor—industrialist, philanthropist, and art collector **Armand G. Hammer** (1898–1990)—the museum is owned by UCLA and operated by the School of Arts and Architecture. Opened in 1990, this museum focuses on works at the cutting edge of the art world in Los Angeles. In addition, it offers free lectures, readings, performances, and films on many nights of the week. The museum is also blessed with a fine permanent collection of contemporary art from the 1960s, the Grunwald Center Collection of art from the Renaissance to the present, and the Daumier Collection of works by French artist and satirist **Honoré Daumier** (1808–1879).

After leaving the Hammer, you may want some lunch. There are many choices in the Village, both quality restaurants and fast food, or at the student cafeteria in Ackerman Union, your next stop.

Walk north on Westwood Boulevard about half a mile, through Westwood Village to Gayley Avenue and the entrance to the **UCLA campus.** Here, Westwood Boulevard morphs into Westwood Plaza. You are on South Campus, locale of the sciences, technology, engineering, and the UCLA Medical Center. Keep walking north to your next destination—the Central Campus—which is devoted to student services and athletics. **Ackerman Union** will be on your right. **Enter through the UCLA Store** (bookstore) **and take the elevator to the cafeteria on the second level.** You are looking for the **mural** ***The Black Experience.*** After you enter the cafeteria, if you don't see it

20

The Black Experience

308 Westwood Plaza

Ackerman Union • UCLA campus

immediately, ask someone to point it out to you. This 10-by-27-foot stunning work of art in black and brown tones was created in 1970 during the Civil Rights/Vietnam War era by seven African American art students at UCLA. It depicts eight young African Americans: three men and five women. These are the faces of leaders in the student civil rights movement, which include **Angela Davis** and **Stokely Carmichael** (1941–1998).[1] The young faces look out at you from another time, with a gaze that is both penetrating and wistful. The portraits make use of the collage technique that incorporates words and photographs. The effect is very moving. It was covered over by a false wall during renovations in 1992, and remained hidden for two decades.[2]

1) The young black leaders were considered controversial at the time, and Angela Davis, a UCLA faculty member, was fired because of her association with the Communist Party and the Black Panther Party.

2) Muralist Judy Baca, UCLA Professor of Art (see Adventure 15), points out that a legacy of censorship that began in 1932—when Siquieros' mural at Olvera Street was whitewashed—still

Good friends heading into the Fowler Museum

In 2012, the Afrikan Student Union brought it to the attention of the Associated Students Board of Directors and it was subsequently uncovered and restored. The mural's reappearance in 2014 created quite a sensation and it has become a well-known landmark.[3]

The food served on the UCLA campus is well regarded, so this is a good choice for lunch. **Restrooms** are located nearby.

Return to Westwood Plaza and continue walking north. You will notice the athletic facilities on your left, home of the UCLA basketball team made famous by coach John Wooden. Soon you will be on North Campus, home of the humanities, art, music, and social sciences, that are housed in the university's original buildings in the beautiful *Romanesque Revival* style, including the **Fowler Museum** on your right. Like the Hammer Museum, the Fowler is also operated by the UCLA School of Arts and Architecture and is famous for its collection

---

haunts Los Angeles (see Adventure 1). She may have been thinking of incidents such as this one in 1992, which hid the mural in Ackerman Union.

3) *Los Angeles Times,* June 7, 2014. "A long hidden mural is revealed, along with a piece of UCLA history," by Jason Song.

Fowler Museum

308 Charles E. Young Drive North
UCLA campus
310-825-4361 • fowler.ucla.edu
Wednesday: 12noon–5:00pm
Thursday: 12noon–8:00pm
Friday, Saturday, Sunday: 12noon–5:00pm
Closed Monday and Tuesday • Check calendar for holiday closures
Admission is Free

of art and textiles from Africa, Asia, the Pacific, and the Americas. It was established in 1963 to house the university's large collection of non-Western art accumulated over many years. In 2006, it was named in recognition of the financial support by the Fowler Foundation and family of collector **Francis E. Fowler, Jr.**[4] The museum has a beautiful

4) Francis E. Fowler was an inventor and collector of ethnic art.

Iconic Royce Hall, opened in 1929

interior, centered around a courtyard and fountain. Rotating exhibits at the Fowler are always wonderfully lively and entertaining, and the museum store is well stocked with colorful items from around the world.

When you come out of the Fowler, take a look to your left (east). You will see a staircase in the distance. These are the famous **Janss Steps,** a feature at UCLA from its very inception. Eighty-seven steps form the gateway to the historic core of the campus, composed of the quad, **Royce Hall** (with its signature pair of towers), and **Powell Library.** It is worth the climb to see them. This area has appeared in a number of Hollywood movies, including *Legally Blonde.*

Walk back to the Village, and make the trek down to Wilshire. When you get to Weyburn Avenue, take a little detour to the right for one block to see the **Fox Village Theatre** (1931) and the **Bruin Theatre** (1937), two siblings in the *Spanish Colonial Revival* style with a touch of *Art Deco Moderne,* that face each other. What could be more LA! Both theatres have been the scene for countless sneak previews and movie premieres over the years.

If you don't want to walk the half mile back to Wilshire, you can catch the **MTA #20 Local** bus on the northwest corner of Gayley Avenue and Westwood Boulevard. Get off at Wilshire and Westwood. Catch the **eastbound #720 Rapid** on the southeast corner. Exit the bus at **Wilshire and Western**, and catch the **Metro Purple Line** back to **Union Station.**

LA
© 2015 Grace E. Moremen

21

LA's First Seaside Resort: Santa Monica

The Santa Monica Pier Marine Education Center

*For this Adventure get an early start, and equip yourself with sandals, a towel, and perhaps a hat. You are heading to the **Pacific Ocean!***

One of the oldest suburbs of Los Angeles, the independent city of Santa Monica was founded on July 15, 1875. Located about eighteen miles west of downtown, Santa Monica's swimming beach and scenic **Palisades Park** have welcomed visitors for generations. Your destination today is the Santa Monica Pier, **Pacific Park Amusement Center**, and the beach.†*

 *1½ miles max*  *5–6 hours*  *minimum*

* *Wilshire Boulevard: Grand Concourse of Los Angeles* by Kevin Roderick and J. Eric Lynxwiler. Angel City Press, 2011.

† Unless otherwise indicated, background information for Adventure 21 comes from the book *Santa Monica Pier: A Century on the Last Great Pleasure Pier*, by James Harris, Angel City Press, 2009.

Before you leave, pack a lunch or buy a sandwich. And be sure to take a bottle of water. From Union Station, take the **Metro Red or Purple Line to Metro Center. Transfer to the Expo Line upstairs.** Don't forget to tap your ticket before boarding. Exit at the end of the Expo Line, which is currently the Culver City Station.[1] Cross Venice Boulevard to the north side and look for the stop for the **#733 Rapid Red bus, direction of Santa Monica.** Get off the bus at the end of the line which terminates at Ocean Avenue.

Immediately after exiting the bus you will notice a welcome "change of air," wafted on a westerly breeze from the ocean, and you will be ready for your mini-vacation at the seashore. **Restrooms** are located nearby in a small building in Palisades Park.

Now walk a short distance south on Ocean Avenue to Colorado Avenue and the entrance to the **Santa Monica Municipal Pier,** a vintage survivor from the once-anticipated "magestic" port of Los Angeles, a port that never materialized.[2] The pier's history can be found on a plaque near the **Hippodrome**:

> The Santa Monica Pier was built in phases between 1908 and 1916. It originally consisted of a Municipal Pier for strolling and fishing and a Pleasure Pier for amusements. The Hippodrome was constructed in 1916 to house the Pleasure Pier's carousel, and is one of the last remnants of a festive architecture once found in most California seaside resort towns. The pier was partially reconstructed between 1988 and 1990 after incurring major storm damage in 1983. It was designated a Santa Monica Historic Landmark in 1975.

What the plaque doesn't say is that the pier's first purpose was not for amusement but to conduct a sewage pipe from the treatment plant out to sea.

As you begin to walk on the pier you will encounter the aforementioned Hippodrome, built by Danish immigrant and master woodcarver **Charles I. D. Looff** (1852–1918), to house his carousel.[3]

---

1) The Expo Line is due to complete its route to Santa Monica by late 2015 or early 2016.
2) San Pedro, to the south, ultimately became the choice to be Port of Los Angeles.
3) Hippodrome means "a stadium for horses" in Greek."

The building's fanciful architecture mixes ***Byzantine, Moorish,*** and ***California*** styles. Completely renovated and restored in 1980–81, the Hippodrome, its carousel horses, and music beckon you to come in and enjoy a ride. You will find that each of the beautifully painted wooden horses has its own charming expression. Pick out your steed and enjoy a jolly ride accompanied by the unique "circus" sound of the Wurlitzer organ. It is one of the few antique wooden merry-go-rounds still operating in the country, and is a "movie star" to boot, having appeared in the Oscar-winning film *The Sting.*[4] It is worth the long ride out to Santa Monica just to experience this carousel. Don't miss it!!

Carousel

Weekdays: 11:00am–7:00pm

Saturdays & Sundays: 11:00am–9:00pm

Closed Tuesdays

Children ages 3–14: $1 • Adults: $2

4) There have been three carousels on the pier. The first was built by Looff, the second was an A.C.W. Parker (#316), and the present one is by the Philadelphia Toboggan Company (#62). It was rediscovered in the 1930s and installed in its present location in 1947.

Santa Monica Pier Aquarium Marine Education Center

1600 Ocean Front Walk

Tuesday-Friday • 2:00pm-6:00pm

Weekends 12:30pm-6:00pm

Free admission for children ages 0-12 • over 12: $5

A short distance beyond the Hippodrome is something that might surprise you: the western terminus for **Route 66**, America's historic cross-country highway that extends from Chicago to Santa Monica. You will see a sign commemorating that highway; it's a good photo opportunity.

To your left is a wider part of the pier that holds the attractive, smallish amusement center called **Pacific Park.** Admission to the park is free, and its thirteen rides are newly refurbished and reasonably priced. They include a bumper-car arena, a medium-sized rollercoaster, and a full-sized, solar–powered Ferris wheel. Alongside this area is **Playland,** an old-time video-game arcade.

Back on the main pier, walk out to the end. There are many souvenir stands, shops, and places to eat along the way, but you will also see people fishing, as it is a good fishing ground.[5] Near the end of the pier is a display of historic photographs telling the story of the pier. There are **Restrooms** nearby.

Walk back toward the beach and look for a staircase (there is one on either side of the pier) that takes you down to the sand. If it's a hot day, keep your sandals on until you reach the water's edge because the sand can be extremely hot on bare feet. By all means go wading in the cool-to-chilly water of the Pacific Ocean—you did not journey all this way only to miss this experience! After a walk and a wade, why not spread out your towel, sit down, and enjoy your sandwich while watching the passing scene?

---

5) A man with a fishing pole once got on a bus that Grace was riding near Hollywood. She asked him where he was going and he replied, "Santa Monica Pier."

If you are so inclined, you can **rent a bicycle** at the back of the beach south of the pier for a reasonable fee and go pedaling along **The Strand,** a paved beachside trail that extends for several miles.

Beneath the pier at the sidewalk level is the **Marine Education Center,** a small aquarium that features local fish and other sea creatures and gives information about the **Santa Monica Bay** and the need to keep it healthy.

There are **Restrooms** located near the aquarium.[6]

For the trip back to downtown LA, exit the pier on Colorado Avenue. The stop for the **MTA #733 Red** bus is on Colorado Avenue about half a block (east) after you cross Ocean Avenue. The **bus ride to the Expo Line Station** takes about 35 minutes. The stop for the station will be announced on the bus. **Take the Expo Line to Metro Center, and transfer to the Red or Purple Line for your return to Union Station.**

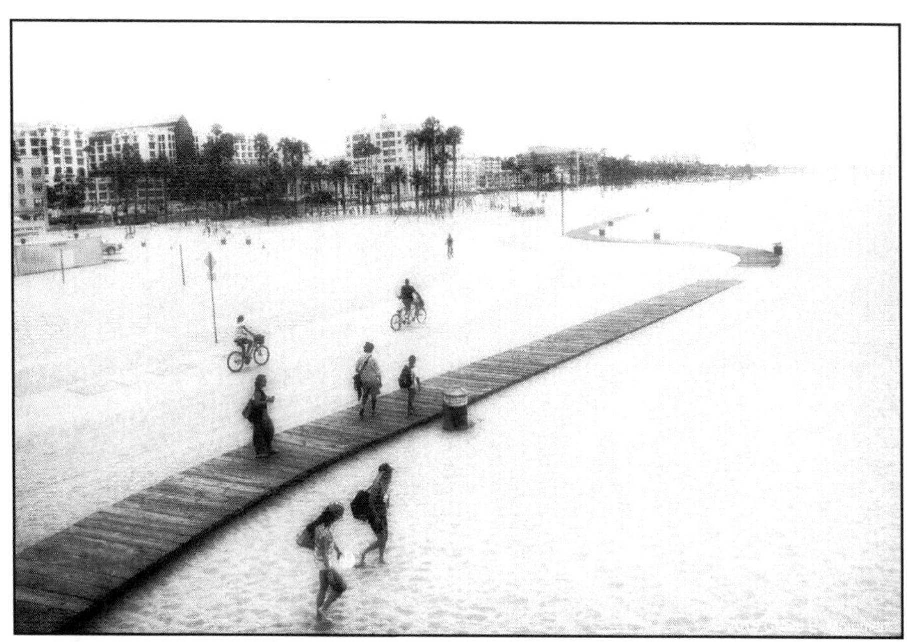

Just south of the pier, looking toward Venice Beach and beyond.

6) For other attractions in Santa Monica go to the city's website: smgov.net

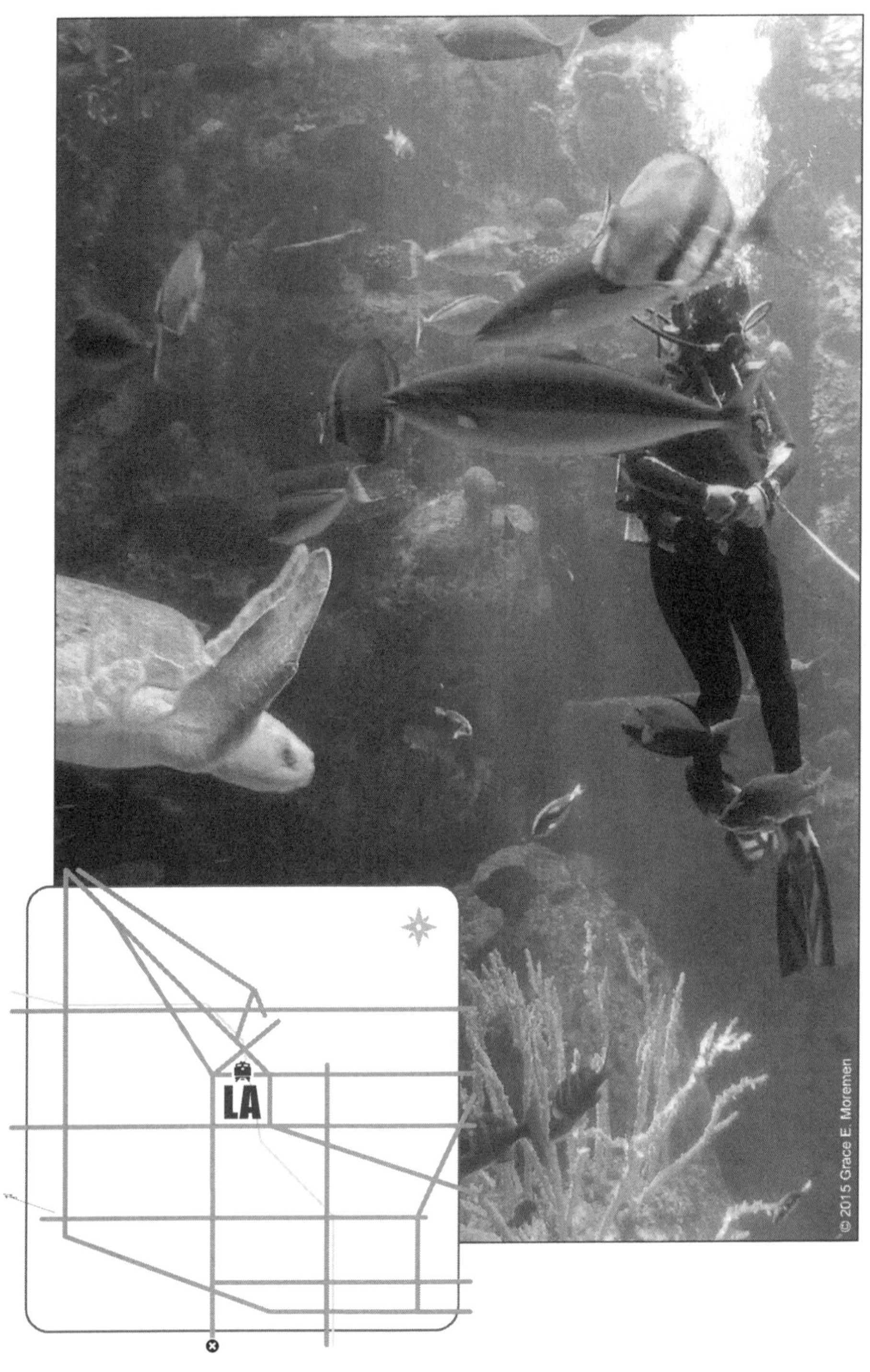
LA

22

For Love of the Ocean: Aquarium of the Pacific

Because of the length of time spent on public transportation for this Adventure, it might be advisable to go by car, especially if you are taking young children. However, the ***Blue Line*** *is direct, more eco-friendly than the freeway, and the scenery is probably more interesting.*

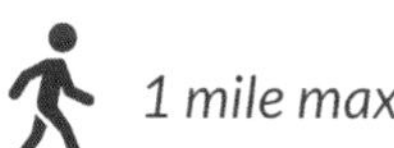

From Union Station take the Red or Purple Metro Line to Seventh Street/Metro Center Station and go upstairs to board the Blue Line; be sure to tap your Metrolink ticket. As you approach the 103rd Street/Watts Towers station, look for the towers off to your left. Another sight to look for is the Del Amo Greenway of the Los Angeles River which features high marsh grasses. You might even see a red-winged blackbird or two.

Get off the train at the end of the line in downtown Long Beach. Walk towards **Ocean Avenue** and look for the **Long Beach Transit Bus (LBTB)** to the aquarium—there is no bus fee.

The mission of the **Aquarium of the Pacific** is "to instill a sense of wonder, respect, and stewardship for the Pacific Ocean, its inhabitants, and ecosystems." There are over 11,000 animals of the Pacific Ocean in more than 50 exhibits—for example, **Ocean Exploration, June Keyes Penguin Habitat, Molina Animal Care Center, Shark Lagoon,** and

A Giant Replica of a Blue Whale hangs from the ceiling in the main lobby.

Whales: Voices of the Sea, to name a few. There are many specialized tours and adventures for children of all ages, such as day camps, school field trips, and sleepovers.

The **outdoor touching pools** containing bat rays, sea stars, and bonnethead sharks are fascinating and very popular as visitors are allowed to touch the animals. The sight of the extraordinarily large stingray may take your breath away. In the **Tropical Reef Habitat,** a diver floats down into the habitat to talk with visitors. The diver wears a special mask and headset with microphone that allows him or her to hear questions and give answers. A large ray might swim by and enjoy a gentle stroking by the diver. This habitat holds 350,000 gallons of seawater with over 1,000 animals and is quite a sight to see and experience.

Among the most impressive features of the aquarium are the **ten-minute presentations at specific exhibits given by well-trained educators.** They are knowledgeable, patient, and very respectful as they encourage questions from the attendees, especially the youngest visitors.

It is enjoyable to watch the playful otters swim, the penguins stroll,

Aquarium of the Pacific

100 Aquarium Way, Long Beach
562-590-3100 • aquariumofpacific.org

Open Daily 9:00am–6:00pm
Closed Christmas Day
and during Grand Prix of Long Beach in April
(Check website for dates)
Adults: $28.95 • Seniors (62+): $25.95 • Child (3–11): $14.95

and the tiny seahorses and sea dragons bob around in their special water environment. You learn interesting bits of information, such as it is the male seahorse who incubates the eggs until they hatch.

One of the favorite exhibits is called **Whales: Voices in the Sea**. Here you can listen to the voices of the humpback, sperm, gray, blue, beaked, and the endangered North Atlantic right whales, watch videos of the whales, and learn about conservation issues and more.

There are so many exhibits to see and experience at the Aquarium that it is advisable to check out the website to plan your visit.

For your return to the Blue Line Station, board the **Long Beach Transit free shuttle in front of the aquarium**. The bus stop is slightly to the right of where you come out. At the station, **Tap your ticket before you board the train.** You will need to **transfer to the Red or Purple Line at Metro Center. Go downstairs and take the train marked "Union Station."**

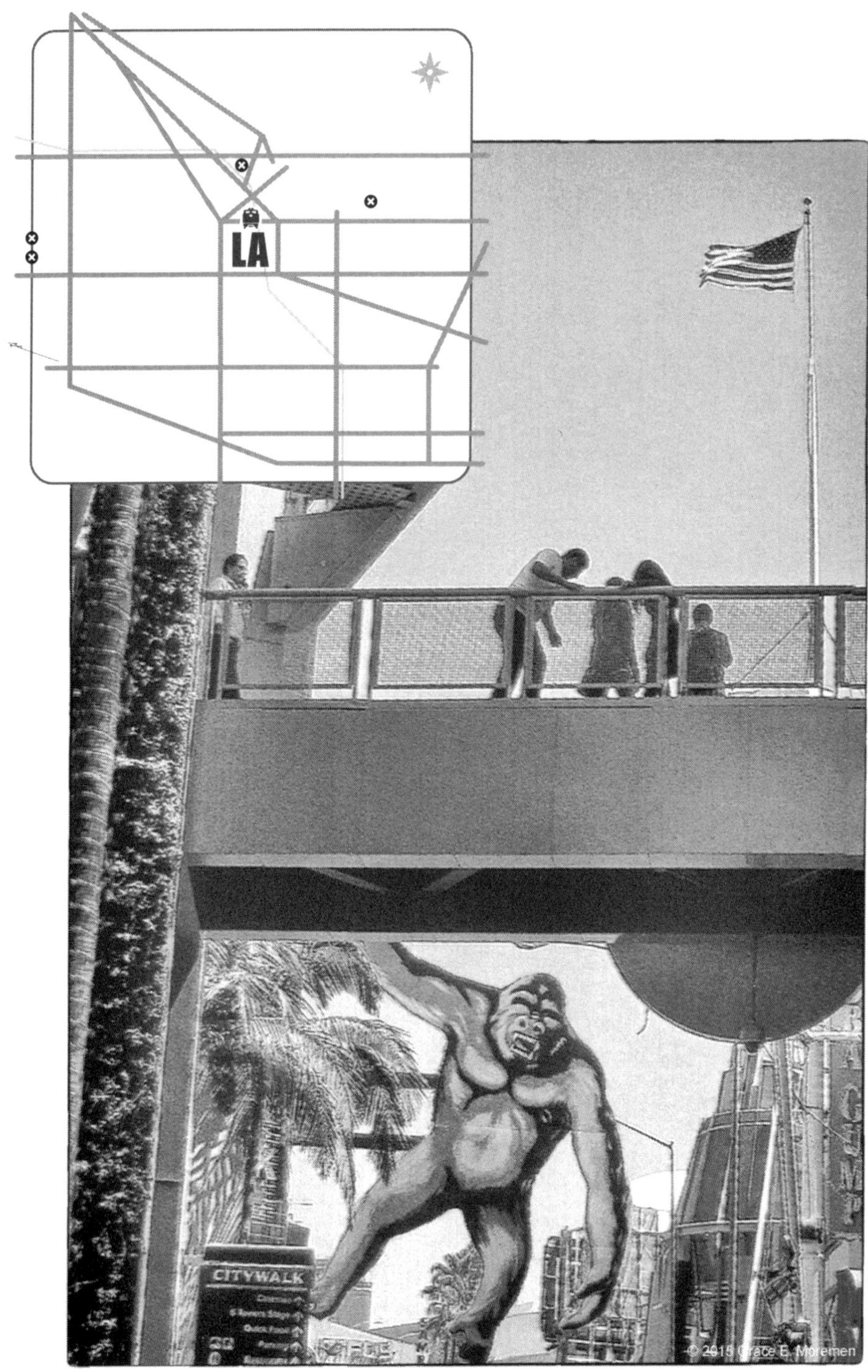
LA
CITYWALK
© 2015 Grace E. Moremen

23

Universal Studios and City Walk

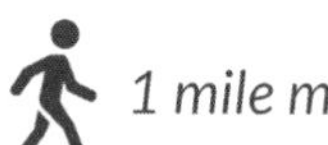

5–6 hours

The Universal Studios complex is located on a mountaintop in the Santa Monica Mountains near Burbank. It is very easy to reach by the ***Metro Red Line*** *from* ***Union Station.*** *Exit at* ***Universal City Station.*** *A* ***free shuttle*** *across the street from the station takes you up the mountain to the gates.**

* Much of the background information for Adventure 23 found on Universal Studios' website.

Universal Studios

800-622-4455 • universalstudioshollywood.com
Hours: Daily opens at 11:00am
Closing times vary with the season.
Cost: there are several different admission packages
Check website for current prices.

Carl Laemmle (1867–1939) founded **Universal Studios** and **Universal City** in 1912 on unincorporated land in the San Fernando Valley. The studio has enjoyed many box office hits over the years—two early ones were *The Hunchback of Notre Dame* in 1923 and *Phantom of the Opera* in 1925, both starring **Lon Chaney** (1883–1930). In recent years, Universal has produced a number of blockbusters including *Jaws, E.T. the Extra Terrestrial*, and *Jurassic Park*. Universal's four-acre back lot is the largest of all **Hollywood** studios and here you have a chance to see much of it. As you progress through the studio tour aboard a tram, you will come face to face with such fearsome creatures as **King Kong** and **Jaws**. While explosions from *War of the Worlds* and the screams of the victim in *Psycho* may give you thrills and chills.

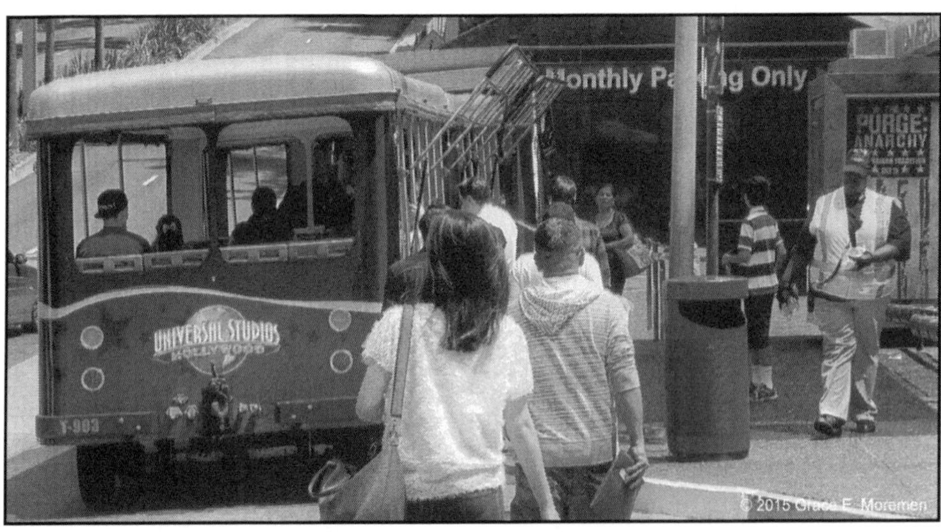

© 2015 Grace E. Moremen

City Walk

Adjacent to the amusement park

An outdoor mall with colorful shops

Live shows and restaurants

From the beginning, Carl Laemmle reached out to the public and offered studio tours, so tours have always been a part of Universal. Eventually, the company decided to add a theme park and an amusement park. In 1962 Universal moved to its present mountaintop location. In 1993, it opened **City Walk**, a three-block-long promenade of restaurants, shops and theaters that leads visitors to the amusement park. Designed by local architect **Jon Jerde** (1940–2015), City Walk has been described as a truly "communal space."[1] We found it to be very people friendly. You may be surprised by the delightful walk-through fountain and fascinated by the pool with ocean waves.

A trip to Universal Studios, because of its easy accessibility by public transportation, is one of the most doable of our Adventures.

Take the subway back to Union Station.

1) *Los Angeles Times*, Section F, March 22, 2015. Jon Jerde was a graduate of the USC School of Architecture and he designed many innovative malls around the country.

LA
© 2015 Grace E. Moremen

24

The Best Bargain in Los Angeles:

Free Rides on LA's Scenic Bus Routes

Now that you are a seasoned traveler in Los Angeles, you are ready to face the final transportation challenge: ***choosing the longer bus ride because it is scenic and/or interesting in itself****, not just because it's a way to get somewhere. If you can take pleasure in that, you have earned an advanced degree in LA Appreciation! Don't be intimidated by public transportation. Remember that your* ***Metrolink ticket*** *or* ***Day Pass*** *or* ***Tap Card*** *allows you to get on and off the bus whenever you wish.* ***Try improvising!*** *You will begin to find that as you increase your experience with the different bus routes, the more it will be possible for you to vary or combine your Adventures. For example, on the way home from a particular Adventure, you might spy a familiar bus and realize that you could take it to a place you have enjoyed before and would like to see again. Mix and match!* ***The following are four rides we recommend...***

Pack a picnic or buy a sandwich. From Union Station take the **Red or Purple Line to Civic Center**. Use the Temple Street/ Grand Park exit. Cross Temple to the northeast corner and look for the sign for the **#92 MTA Local** (orange) bus. The bus will be marked **"Burbank Station via Glendale."** It is very important to get a **window seat on the right side of the bus facing forward** because you

24A: The Museum of Neon Art and Glendale via Echo Park and the Hyperion Bridge

For an interesting journey that takes you northeast from downtown LA, across the river, to the foot of the San Gabriel Mountains, ride the bus to Glendale! The Museum of Neon Art has recently relocated there, a sparkling centerpiece for your visit.

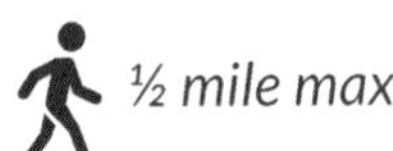

will be passing by **Echo Park Lake.** If you have already visited this lovely lake (Adventure 16), you know that it is only a ten-minute ride from downtown.[1]

After passing over the Hollywood Freeway, the bus skims the southern edge of **Angeleno Heights**, famous for its old Victorian houses, before it turns onto Glendale Boulevard. When the **lake comes into view on your right you'll see the luscious spread of water lilies,** and in summer the long-stemmed lotus blossums shine as the bus follows the entire length of the park.

Continuing on Glendale Blvd., you can't miss the **Angelus Temple** on your right just after you leave the park. It was opened on January 1, 1923 as the Four Square Gospel Church by the famous evangelist, **Aimee Semple McPherson** (1890–1944).

Did you know that some of the earliest silent movies in Los Angeles were filmed in the Echo Park district, then called "Edendale"? In 1912, **Mack Sennett** (1880–1960) established his **Keystone Studio** at what is now 1712 Glendale Boulevard, a few blocks north of Echo Park Lake.

---

1) Background information for MONA is from the Neon Museum website and the Neon Cruise.

Here **Charlie Chaplin** (1889–1977) cavorted as the 'Little Tramp,' and the **Keystone Cops** romped through the neighborhood in pursuit of the usual suspects. Sennett's original building still stands, but it is now a public storage facility. The #92 bus passes very near it.

The next neighborhood you pass through is the **Silver Lake District.** Like Echo Park, Silver Lake is a popular bedroom community that is developing economically. After about fifteen minutes you will come to Riverside Drive and the **Hyperion Bridge** (1929). One of the "City Beautiful" bridges over the Los Angeles River, it is the link between LA/Hollywood and the independent city of **Glendale.** A number of early movies made use of the bridge, and its lights appear in a night scene in the 1944 film noir, *Double Indemnity.* The bus travels over the bridge, follows Glendale Boulevard east, goes under the Amtrak railroad tracks and turns left (north) onto Brand Boulevard that leads to downtown Glendale. The scenery is quite nice here, graced by tall palm trees with the purple-gray San Gabriel Mountains in the near distance.

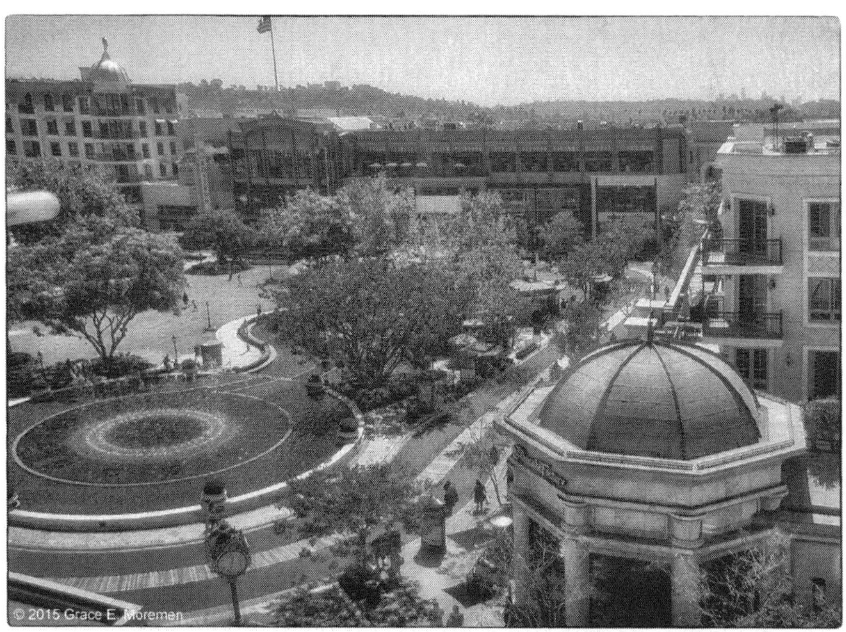

Looking toward downtown Los Angeles from the 'Americana,' Glendale

Museum of Neon Art (MONA)

216 South Brand Boulevard, Glendale

213-489-9918 • neonmona.org • (opening late 2015)

Neon Cruise: $55 • $45 for members

Founded in 1887, Glendale is situated on land that was once the Verdugo Rancho. It is one of the oldest suburbs of Los Angeles. Exit the bus at Colorado Street. **The Museum of Neon Art (MONA)** is a little way farther north on your right. Look for the figure of a diver outlined in neon atop the building. MONA is the only museum in the world devoted solely to "art that incorporates neon lighting, including the preservation of old neon signs, as well as displaying original fine art and kinetic art." MONA conducts Saturday night "Neon Cruises" of Los Angeles (on an open double-decker bus) from June to September (Adventure 13). The cruises are fun and informative. See the city at night! To learn more go to their website: neonMONA.org

The Americana Mall, opened in 2008, is across the street from MONA. The best access is from **Harvard Street**. It is reminiscent of "The Grove" near Farmers Market in LA, as both were built by the same developer. There is a lovely interior park with a lake, fountains, and waterfalls. Blankets are available for you to spread on the grass to rest and eat your lunch. A nice feature of the Americana is the outside elevator. At no cost, you can go up to the top (8th) floor for a dramatic, panoramic view in each direction: to the south, the skyline of downtown Los Angeles; to the west, the Santa Monica Mountains and Griffith Park; to the north, the flat plain of the San Fernando Valley: and to the east, the San Gabriel Mountains. It is a unique opportunity to view the Los Angeles basin from a northern perspective, and well worth the quick elevator ride. If you walk through the Americana, you will come out on Central Avenue. Across the street is the **Glendale Galleria**, which opened in 1976. The Galleria is an indoor, more traditional mall. It has **Restrooms**, and there is a Starbucks located in the Target deparment store.

To vary your return trip, catch a **#794 Rapid Bus** on Central, in front of the Galleria. **Exit at Hollywood Blvd./Western Ave.** intersection, go into the **Red Line Metro Station for your trip back to Union Station**.

© 2015 Grace E.

24B: A Trip to the San Gabriel Mission via the scenic Gold Line

In the late summer of 1781 this mission sheltered and fed a party of forty-four ***Pobladores*** *(settlers) for several weeks, due to the illness of one member of the party. When they continued on their way, they established the* ***Pueblo de los Angeles****. Remarkably well preserved, the mission stands today in a beautiful park-like setting for the public to visit.*

 *1 mile max*  *3 hours*  *no fees*

The **Mission San Gabriel Arcángel** is only eight miles from downtown Los Angeles, and it played an important role in the founding of the city.

Bring a sandwich or buy one at Union Station. Be sure and pick up a schedule for the MTA **Local #176** bus at the east end of Union Station. Take the **Gold Line, direction "Sierra Madre."** The fifteen-minute ride is pleasant and scenic as you travel via the Arroyo Seco with its plentiful sycamores and hilly landscapes (see Adventure 18). **Get off at the South Pasadena Station,** cross the tracks to your left, and look for the sign for the **#176 Bus on Mission Street.** The bus ride goes through some attractive cityscapes and residential neighborhoods in **South Pasadena, Alhambra, and San Gabriel.**

* Much of the information for Wilshire Boulevard comes from the book *Wilshire Boulevard: Grand Concourse of Los Angeles*, by Kevin Roderick and Eric Lynxwiler; and *Los Angeles: An Architectural Guide*, by Gebhard and Winter.

Mission San Gabriel Arcángel

537 W. Mission Drive
San Gabriel
626-457-3035
Guided tours daily: inquire in gift shop

Exit the bus at Santa Anita Avenue and Broadway. The Mission is straight ahead about three blocks. Stay to the left. You will pass the San Gabriel Playhouse. Keep going. You will see the **mission buildings on your left.** Keep walking to your left past the bell wall and around to the front of the church. This fortress-like building has the look of *Moorish* architecture and is unlike any of the other California mission churches.[2]

Look for the entrance to the mission grounds through the gift shop. And that is where the guided tours start. Maps are available in the gift shop, also.

The inside of the church resembles other missions, but it is unique in the fact that the building and its contents have been so well preserved over the centuries. Its original small baptistry with a domed ceiling is adjacent to the sanctuary. It contains a hand-hammered copper font given to the Mission in the 1790s by **King Carlos III of Spain** (1714–1788). The paintings mounted on the wall of the sanctuary date from that time also, as does the high pulpit. A 300-year-old painting of "Our Lady of Sorrows," to the left of the altar, has a very interesting history, which you will learn. In the large museum behind the church are many other significant works of art and artifacts.

Founded in 1771, Mission San Gabriel Arcángel was fourth in the establishment of the twenty-one California missions. Over the years, its location at a crossroads made it an important hub for travelers. The native Tongva people in the surrounding area, many of whom con-

2) From the leaflet "Mission San Gabriel," 2014, provided by the mission.
* Major background information for the San Gabriel Mission can be found in the book *Mission San Gabriel Arcángel* by Mary Null Boule. Merryant Publishers, 1988.

verted to Christianity, were brought in as laborers and were given the name *Gabrieleños*. Many thousands are buried in the Mission cemetery; a monument has been erected to their memory. The Mission's patio, where once the production of soap and candles took place, has been preserved. **Junipero Serra's** (1713–1784) last surviving associate, **Father Sanchez**, is buried in the church along with his colleague **Father Cruzado**. Both died in 1805. Together they served the San Gabriel Mission for almost thirty years, from 1776 to 1805.

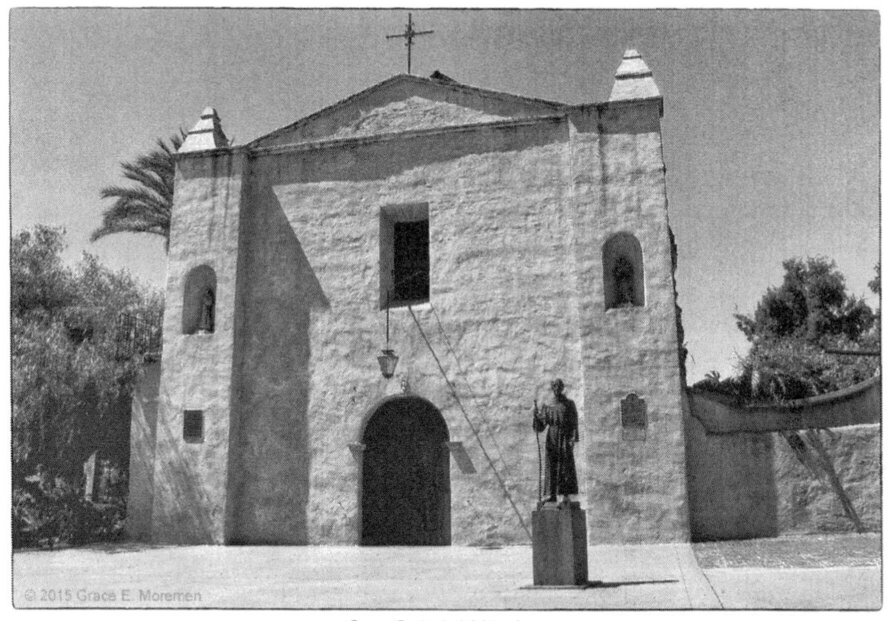

San Gabriel Mission

For your return, check the #176 schedule for the bus's westbound arrival time at Santa Anita and Broadway. Walk back along Santa Anita Avenue to the bus stop (across from where you got off).

Exit the bus at the **Gold Line Station** and take a **southbound train, marked "East LA," back to Union Station.**

24C: Wilshire Boulevard to Santa Monica

This is a true LA lover's ride. Be flexible. Get off the bus when you like and back on when you like. Just remember that the ***Rapid buses only stop at major intersections.*** *The buses are often less crowded from 9:30am to 2:30pm.**

 *1½ miles max*  *5–6 hours*  *no fees*

From Union Station take the **Metro Purple Line to the end of the line, the Wilshire/ Western Station. Transfer to the #720 Rapid Red bus on Wilshire Boulevard.**

Or, you can board the #720 downtown, near the Pershing Square Metro Station, on Fifth Street between Broadway and Hill Street.

Wilshire is LA's classiest thoroughfare. But at the turn of the twentieth century, beyond Westlake Park, the road that would become Wilshire Boulevard was scarcely more than a track over fields of barley. It had only one landmark: the **La Brea Tar Pits**. By the 1920s, Wilshire had become a spacious roadway and "the" residential address for the social set. Today most of those mansions are gone, but happily many of the commercial buildings that replaced them are beautiful examples of *Art Deco* and *Moderne* styles, and have historic landmark status.

The advantage of catching the #720 Rapid bus downtown is that you will get to see **MacArthur Park** (1880s), formerly "Westlake Park" and <u>on your left,</u> **Bullocks Wilshire Department Store** (1929), now the Southwestern School of Law, **an *Art Deco* masterpiece designed by John and Donald Parkinson.**

May Company Building/LACMA on Wilshire Boulevard

At Wilshire and Western Avenue admire the **Pellissier Building** and **Wiltern Theatre** (1931) <u>on your left</u>, **considered to be the most outstanding example of *Art Deco* in the United States.** The building encompasses an entire block, and is covered in glazed blue-green terra cotta tiles in a *zig-zag moderne* design. If you came by way of the Metro Purple Line

Art Moderne-style retail building on Wilshire Boulevard

and are waiting for the #720 bus, take time to cross Wilshire and **look at the ceiling of the Wiltern Theatre's box office lobby.** You will be stunned by the beauty of the **magnificent pale gray starburst design.** It is one of many treasures in Los Angeles hiding in plain sight.[3] Don't worry about missing a bus, the Rapid #720 runs frequently. **Just be sure you catch one marked "Santa Monica."**

Back on the #720 you will now be in the **mid-Wilshire district**, home to a very large Korean population. The **Consulate of the Republic of South Korea** is located at 3243 Wilshire. Soon you will be in **Hancock Park,** an affluent neighborhood that extends along Wilshire between Western and La Brea Avenue. Notice on your right the succession of curving, tree-lined streets and large, attractive homes. A number of distinguished churches and the **Wilshire Boulevard Temple** (1929) are located in this neighborhood. Farther along, you may spot, on your left the *classical*-style **Wilshire Ebell Theater** (1927) at Wilshire and S. Lucerne Boulevard. Here **Judy Garland** (1922–1969) was discovered, and **Amelia Earhart** (1897–1937) made her last public appearance.

3) Our book's cover art features a Rapid Bus fancifully 'parked' on this dynamic ceiling design.

If you want to be adventurous, **exit the bus at La Brea Avenue** and walk the **"Miracle Mile"** to see, up close, the wealth of landmarks. But first, take time to walk back a short distance (east) to look at the one-story building, formerly the **Security Pacific National Bank** (1937). It is an *Art Deco*-style gem covered in black glazed terra cotta tile in a zig-zag pattern with gold accents. Next door, on the corner, is the multi-story **E. Clem Wilson building** (1929), also bearing *Art Deco*-style details.

As you proceed, notice the **Staples** store at 5407 Wilshire, a perfect example of the ***Art Moderne*** style (1937). Farther on you will see the *Art Deco*-style **El Rey Theater** at 5515 Wilshire (1936), with its terrazzo floor in beautiful 1930s stylized flowers and clouds.

If it is Wednesday, there will be several blocks of **food trucks** on the south side of Wilshire opposite Museum Square, formerly the Prudential Building (1948). This might be a good place to buy some lunch. **The Tar Pits** and the **LA County Museum of Art (LACMA)** come next on your right (see Adventures 7 and 8). The Miracle Mile ends at Wilshire and Fairfax Avenue where, on the northeast corner, stands the former **May Company Wilshire Department Store** (1939–1940), with its golden "silo" flanked by two black columns. Designed by **Albert C. Martin, Jr.** (1879–1960),[4] it has been called the greatest surviving example of *Streamline Modern* in Los Angeles.[5] On the northwest corner, across from the May Company building, don't overlook **Johnie's Coffee Shop** (1956) designed by architects **Louis Armét** and **Eldon C. Davis.** (Their firm is has been called "the Frank Lloyd Wright of coffee shops.") Johnie's whimsical, outlandish design represents the *Googie* style (a subdivision of *Futuristic* or *Doo Wop* architecture) that originated in Southern California and flourished from the mid-1940s to the mid-1960s. In those years, it was the style of choice not only for coffee shops but also motels, bowling alleys, theaters, and gas stations—places

4) Martin was also one of the architects of City Hall.

5) So designated by the LA Conservancy. Now owned by LACMA, it is the future home of the Academy of Motion Picture Arts and Sciences, due to open in 2017.

Johnie's Coffee Shop (*do not try to eat there!*) on Wilshire Boulevard

that wanted to attract the attention of passing motorists. The name derives from **Googie's Coffee Shop** that once stood in West Hollywood designed by **John Lautner.** Only recently has the value of these buildings been recognized by historians. A few remain in Hollywood, such as the Capitol Records cylindrical-shaped building (1956) on Vine Street, the Cinerama Dome (1963) on Sunset Blvd., and Norms Restaurant on La Cienega Blvd.[6] But sadly, most of the original "Googies" have been demolished to make room for office buildings.

On the southeast corner of Wilshire and Fairfax stands one of the most striking museum buildings in Los Angeles, the newly refurbished **Petersen Automotive Museum,** due to reopen in November 2015 (Adventure 8).

At Fairfax get back on the westbound Rapid Red #720, destination "Santa Monica," to continue your journey. You will go through the city of **Beverly Hills.** The historic **Beverly Wilshire Hotel** (*Italian Renaissance* style, 1928) at 9500 Wilshire will appear on your left. A favorite corner of ours is where **Wilshire crosses Santa Monica Boulevard. The fountain** (1931) on your right was designed by American sculptor **Robert Merrell Gage** (1892–1981). An early example of an electrically programmed fountain, the water goes through a cycle of different heights, and at night it is lighted by a cycle of changing colors. Grace

6) Gebhard and Winter, *Los Angeles, an Architectural Guide.*

loved to watch it as a child (and still does).[7]

Between Beverly Hills and Westwood at 10101 Wilshire tall fences and hedges screen the **Los Angeles Country Club** (1887) from view. But if you stay alert, you can catch glimpses of the elegantly landscaped golf course that seems to extend for miles on either side of the boulevard.

The bus will travel through **Westwood, home of UCLA**, but you cannot see the campus from Wilshire. Soon after you cross Westwood Boulevard, you will pass the multi-storied **United States Federal Building** on your left, scene of many sociopolitical demonstrations in recent years. After crossing under the 405 Freeway, you will be in **West Los Angeles,** and you'll traverse the grounds of the old **Soldiers Home** (1888) on your right. It was established for veterans of the Civil War, and today encompasses a National Cemetery and a Veterans' Hospital. On your right, be on the lookout for the *Victorian Gothic*-style **Wadsworth Chapel** (1900), the oldest building still standing on Wilshire Boulevard. It is in the National Register of Historic Places.

In about two miles, you enter the city of **Santa Monica** (see Adventure 21). When the bus reaches **Palisades Park,** as it turns onto Ocean Avenue, watch for the welcoming **statue of Saint Monica,** sculpted by **Eugene Morahan** (1869–1949) for the **Works Progress Authority (WPA)** in 1934. Exit the bus here. There are public **Restrooms** in Palisades Park. While you are in Santa Monica, you might want to check out the **Third Street Promenade between Wilshire and Colorado Avenue,** a popular and trendy stretch two blocks in from the park.

For a faster return trip to Union Station (thirty minutes to an hour faster) **catch the Rapid #733 bus. The bus stop is on the south side of Colorado Street, a little east of Ocean Avenue.** After about a thirty-minute ride, you will come to the **Expo Line Culver City Station.** Get off the bus here and catch the **Expo Line to Metro Center. Go downstairs and take the train to Union Station.**

---

7) Grace remembers watching the fountain at night with her brother Robert, looking out the back window of the car, and keeping its vibrant colors in their sight as long as possible as they drove away. (This was before seat belts!)

24-D. Sunset Boulevard to the Pacific Coast Highway

Don't be put off by the length of this trip. If you were driving, it would probably take about the same amount of time, and you would be fighting traffic. This way you can sit back, relax and enjoy the most scenic ride in Los Angeles.

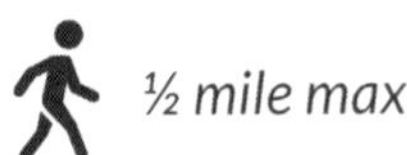
 *6-7 hours*

no fees

If Wilshire is the classiest boulevard in LA, Sunset is the most scenic. It is also one of the city's longest thoroughfares. Sunset Boulevard provides a real slice of LA life, from the mundane to the luxurious, from urban to suburban, and from the mountains to the sea. Pack a lunch or buy a sandwich at Union Station. Take a towel to dry your feet if you decide to wade in the Pacific. **Pick up a schedule for the #2 or #302 MTA Local bus at the east end of Union Station.**

Take the **Red Line to the Vermont /Sunset Station,** a journey of about twenty minutes.[8] **Catch the #2 or the #302 Local** (orange) **bus on Sunset. It will be marked "Pacific Coast Highway" or "PCH." Try to find a window seat near the front on the right side of the bus facing forward.** The ride through Hollywood can be slow but that gives time to notice some landmarks such as the **Palladium Theatre** (*Art Deco* style, 1931) on the right, the **Cinerama Dome Theater** (*Googie* style, 1963) on the left, and farther along on the right, the uplifted globe of **Crossroads,** an innovative outdoor mall from 1936.[9]

8) There is a Restroom in Vons/Starbucks across the street.

9) Crossroads is on the National Register of Historic Places, and is a Los Angeles Historic Cultural Monument.

Emerging from the Metro Station at Vermont & Sunset

In **West Hollywood**, up on the hill to your right, be prepared to glimpse the **Chateau Marmont** (opened 1929), a luxury apartment hotel with long-time connections to the movie industry and movie stars. It was designated an LA Historic Cultural Landmark in 1976.

Sunset Boulevard hugs the hillside as it follows the colorful **Sunset Strip** with its night clubs, cafés, and elegant boutiques. Then, you enter **Beverly Hills** (incorporated in 1914). Notice the mansions that come into view. Not surprisingly, some of your fellow bus riders could be tourists or domestic workers. Their destinations could be the same: to look at or work in the big houses where celebrities live or the swanky and historic **Beverly Hills Hotel** (1912). You will see the hotel on your right, along a winding street lined with the tallest palm trees imaginable,[10] and a little farther, on your right, you will pass by the gates to the exclusive neighborhood of **Bel Air** (1923).[11]

10) A pink "fantasy fit for a movie," according to its website. It has long been a favorite venue for movie stars and royalty. It was completely renovated from 1992 to 1995.

11) Neighborhood of the rich and famous, including the late President Ronald Reagan.

Beverly Hills Hotel, as seen through the window of the bus.

Soon after that, the bus turns off Sunset to wend its way through **Westwood Village** and the **UCLA campus** (Adventure 20), and makes a stop not far from the **UCLA Medical Center** (founded 1955).

The communities of **Brentwood** and **Pacific Palisades** come next, and a series of deep and delicious downward curves through the Santa Monica Mountains as Sunset Boulevard descends to the sea and the **Pacific Coast Highway**.

Get off at the end of the line. **Will Rogers State Beach** is located directly across the highway.[12] There are **Restrooms** in a Taco Bell, in a supermarket/Starbucks nearby, as well as on the beach. Cross the highway at the light and walk down to the shore. It has been a long ride out here, but being able to breathe the fresh sea air away from the city,

12) You will have passed the home of **Will Rogers** (beloved movie actor 1879–1935), located in Pacific Palisades just north of Sunset Boulevard. It is open to the public and you might want to stop off and see it. Ask the bus driver to tell you the correct stop.

makes it worth the effort. And, you have seen some choice scenery along the way. We suggest eating your picnic sitting on the rocks while contemplating the rolling surf and the birds.[13] Maybe you will see a squadron of pelicans flying in gentle formation, or even diving for fish. This beach is in **Pacific Palisades,** while trendy **Malibu Beach** is only a mile or so farther north. If time permits, it's a nice beach for walking and wading.

Check your bus schedule for your return trip. **Get off the bus at Sunset and Vermont; catch the Red Line back to Union Station.**

Will Rogers State Beach, at the end of Sunset Boulevard

13) If you want to eat lunch at a restaurant, there is a good one right where you are, on the beach.

The Adventures Continue…

LovingLA.com

Your mountains and your seacoast

Your folks of every hue,

City of the Angels

I will come back to you.

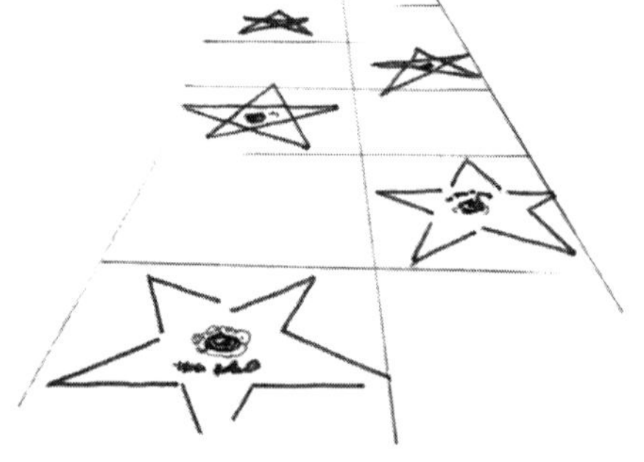

Made in the USA
San Bernardino, CA
03 May 2015